Preparing for a Family Law Case

Money-Saving Tips and Options for Divorce and More

First Edition, Version 1.3

Bryan C. Ginter, J.D.

NOTICES

Copyright Notice

Notice of Liability

be caused directly or indirectly by the information contained in this book.

The information contained in this book is only informational and/or of opinion. The subject matter and applicable law discussed in this book is in a constant state of flux, and legal citations relate to California law only. It is the reader's responsibility to consult with a competent attorney in the reader's jurisdiction before taking any action based on information contained in this book. No legal advice is given and no attorney/client or other relationship is established or intended. Reading or replying to email or accepting or returning telephone calls shall not be considered legal advice and such acts do not form any attorney/client relationship or any other professional relationship.

The information provided is based on experience and the experiences of others as reported. There are no representations, guarantees or warranties that the information contained in this book is accurate and/or appropriate for the usage of any specific reader or situation. Cross links are suggestive only, and there are no warranties of accuracy, applicability or competency.

As of the writing of this book, the author is licensed in California by the State Bar of California. While most of the content in this book can be applied to any state, legal references and citations in this book, including statutes, relate only to California law. If you live in a state other than California, you must consult with an attorney in your area for specific laws that apply to you. Even if you reside in California, you should consult with an attorney to determine your local laws and practices.

Some states may require the wording "This is an advertisement"; to this end, the information in this book is in the nature of an advertisement. The content of this book may be fact-specific and dependent upon the special needs and purposes of the reader. Each situation stands on its own. Readers of this book should consult with their own counsel concerning legal and/or ethical issues for any family law issue they are facing.

Trademarks

Many of the designations used by manufacturers and sellers to distinguish their products are claimed as trademarks. Where those designations appear in this book, and the author was aware of a trademark claim, the designations appear as requested by the owner of the trademark. All other product names and services identified throughout this book are used in editorial fashion only and for the benefit of such companies with no intention of infringement of the trademark. No such use, or the use of any trade name, is intended to convey endorsement or other affiliation with this book.

TABLE OF CONTENTS

DEDICATION

This book is dedicated to the many people facing a family law issue that do not know where to start. This book serves as an introductory guide to educate you with the available options to resolve a family law issue, as well as some practical and money-saving tips along the way.

ACKNOWLEDGMENTS

Special thanks to my mother for the tremendous support she provided during the creation of this book. Thanks to my mother and father, my wife, my two daughters, my brother and my dear friend Dan who consistently give me their love and support. I also wish to thank all of the people that have touched my life—knowingly or not—who gave me the courage, experience and desire to write this book.

ABOUT THE AUTHOR

Bryan C. Ginter is a California family law attorney and mediator. Mr. Ginter owns Ginter Family Law, a law firm based out of Northern California. Mr. Ginter received his Bachelors of Science in Business Management in 1995 from Quinnipiac University, located in Hamden, Connecticut, and then went on to receive his Juris Doctor in 2004 from McGeorge School of Law, located in Sacramento, California. Since 2006, Mr. Ginter has limited his law practice to only family law.

Early in his family law career, Mr. Ginter became trained in, and started practicing, non-adversarial (out-of-court) methods for resolving family law disputes, including such matters as divorce, legal separation, child custody, child support, spousal support, and property division. In addition to receiving many hours of training in litigation, collaborative law and mediation, Mr. Ginter held the position of vice co-chair of the Sacramento Pro Bono Mediation Group (now disbanded) and he has guest-lectured at Sacramento State University on the topic of mediation.

Bryan C. Ginter, J.D.

For more information about Bryan C. Ginter, J.D. and Ginter Family Law, as well as helpful family law resources, visit **www.GinterFamilyLaw.com**.

PREFACE

Maybe you are thinking about a divorce or a **legal separation**. Maybe you know of someone who is having challenges over child custody and when each parent may spend time with minor children. Regardless of the family law issue that is being faced, most of the time there are several options parties have in resolving their **matter**: Should you hire a mediator or an attorney? How do you find a mediator or attorney that will be a good fit for your case? Should you bring your case into court, or should you try to resolve your case out of court? Are there steps that can be taken to help keep costs down? This book was written to answer these questions and more.

Hello. I am California family law attorney and mediator, Bryan C. Ginter. More information about my family law practice and me can be found in the section titled *"About the Author,"* and by visiting **www.GinterFamilyLaw.com**. I will present some of the options available to you for most family law issues—including divorce—and what the differences are between those options so you can make an informed decision on how you would like to approach resolving your case. Additionally, along the way, I will provide tips and tools to help you on your journey. Like most things in life, your journey into making a decision starts with information and education. It is my hope that I can be a guide and a teacher to help you in your endeavor.

You may be wondering why I wrote this book. The information found in this book is oftentimes discussed in a consultation with an attorney…a consultation that can cost *hundreds* of dollars. In California, a very high percentage of people undergoing a family law issue represent themselves. Self-representation oftentimes leads to problems down the line: People make uninformed decisions, legal paperwork is not filled out correctly, and adverse consequences occur because of not understanding the legal process or the law itself.

One of the critical decisions people need to make in their case is *how* they will resolve their case, and many times people do not know the options available to them. I thought about how I could provide a low-cost alternative to people that are facing family law issues to (i) help them make informed decisions about *how* they can resolve their case, (ii) provide practical information on selecting a mediator or attorney, (iii) explain how **retainers** work, and (iv) provide helpful tips in order to reduce **costs**. Hence, I created this book.

Typically, a **party** does not say that he or she *wants* to go to court and have a judge decide the outcome of the case, to spend a lot of money, to have their case drag on for years, to emotionally and financially devastate the other party, and to have the case be fair to him/her and unfair to the other party. Instead, most of the time people say they want the opposite: To *not* go to court, to craft *their own* outcome, to spend *as little* time and money as possible on the case, and to have the outcome be fair for *both* **parties**. Since most people want the latter option, the focus of this book is on *out-of-court* (**non-adversarial**) methods of resolution, including **collaborative law** and **mediation**.

In order to make an educated and informed decision though, one must also understand the in-court (**adversarial**) method, and to understand the differences between collaborative law and mediation. These options will be discussed in detail. Along the way, you will also hear tips and tools to help your family law matter go as smoothly as possible, and to help keep costs down.

A Note about Cited Codes

Unless otherwise indicated, all referenced **statutes** are from the *California* codes. Unless otherwise stated, a **code** section refers to the California Family Code. For example, if you see "Section 2100," this refers to California Family Code Section 2100. As another example, if you see "Code of Civil Procedure Section 1013," this refers to California Code of Civil Procedure Section 1013.

Glossary

At the end of this book, you will find an extensive glossary that defines many of the terms that are recited. Most of the glossary terms used in this book are in bold type to give you notice that there is a definition for that word in the glossary. Therefore, if you see a word in bold, chances are there is a definition for that word in the glossary that you can reference any time you wish.

Reading through This Book

This book can be read through from start to finish. Alternatively, you may use this book as a reference manual and simply skip to the sections that interest you. If you read this book from start to finish, you will likely see some repeated information. This was done intentionally to allow readers the flexibility of using this book as a reference manual such that each section may stand on its own without the requirement of reading the prior sections to understand a current section.

So then, fasten your seat belts, and let's drive through the options in resolving family law matters and learn some helpful tips along the way!

CHAPTER ONE: DIVORCE – A COMMON CASE

Since a **dissolution of marriage** (i.e., a divorce) is one of the most common family law actions, this section will provide some background on the grounds for a divorce in California, and how the understanding of **irreconcilable differences** impacts the approach to resolving the divorce. If your case does not involve a divorce, feel free to skip ahead to the next chapter.

Grounds for a Divorce

A divorce in California can only be supported by two available grounds: (1) Incurable insanity or (2) irreconcilable differences. A clear majority of all divorces in California are based on irreconcilable differences. Any time a divorce is mentioned in this book, it will be based on irreconcilable differences. Incurable insanity is beyond the scope of this book.

Most people have heard the term irreconcilable differences. However, what is it, exactly? If the phrase "irreconcilable differences" were to be summed up as a question asked by the court, it would be this: "When, in *either one* of the parties' minds, was the marriage over with absolutely no chance of repair?" Notice the phrase "either one of the parties' minds." Therefore, obtaining a divorce is not like dancing, where you need "two to tango." Instead, there only needs to be *one* party that wants the divorce for it to occur. To put it another way, to qualify for a divorce based on irreconcilable differences, the marriage only needs to be over in *one* person's mind.

Some people may be saying: "But what if the other person is at fault? It's not *my* fault the marriage is over! Can I use the other person's fault to block the divorce or to support my case to gain an advantage over the other party?" In California, the answer is "no." California has been a "no fault" state for some time now. Therefore, "fault" does *not* need to be shown to prove irreconcilable differences. Fault cannot be used as a sword (i.e., to attack the other party) nor can fault be used as a shield (i.e., as a defense against the other party) in a California divorce action.

It is common for people to believe that infidelity can be used against the other spouse…to claim that the straying spouse is "at fault." While such behavior may not be considered moral or "fair," infidelity cannot be claimed for purposes of irreconcilable differences. Instead, irreconcilable differences can be based off almost anything…a general loss of feelings, different parenting styles, constant disagreements, not liking the other party's hairstyle (well, maybe not this…), and the list goes on. You get the point.

Note that the question of whether there are irreconcilable differences is a subjective question, not an objective one. In other words, the question of irreconcilable differences lies in someone's mind, which makes contesting irreconcilable differences nearly impossible. This being said, someone can attempt to claim that the marriage is salvageable; but, for the most part, all that the other party would need to do is make a few statements while under oath to put the issue to rest and prove irreconcilable differences. Therefore, contesting irreconcilable differences is typically futile.

What If The Other Party Doesn't Want A Divorce?

Oftentimes, one party desires a divorce (let's call this person the *initiator*), and the other party does not (let's call this person the *defender*). It is emotionally difficult enough to traverse through a divorce action where *both* parties wish to divorce. However, where only *one* party is looking to divorce, the emotional trauma on everyone involved, including children, is typically much greater.

In addition to increased emotional difficulties, there is a danger that the defender will attempt to fight against the divorce occurring. This type of sabotage can be done passively or aggressively, unconsciously or subconsciously. For example, a *passive* sabotaging effort is when one party attempts to carry on private conversations with the other party in an attempt to woo him/her back into the marriage. An example of an *aggressive* sabotaging effort is when a party intentionally does not fully disclose some aspect of the financial picture, such as income or the failure to disclose the existence of various assets, including bank accounts or a car.

With any type of sabotaging effort, the divorce process can become painstakingly long, and it can also become extremely financially tolling on the entire family. A party's lack of cooperation almost surely will lead to increased legal **fees** and **costs**. The following are examples of actions that increase fees and costs because of lack of cooperation between the parties: (i) additional legal documentation being filed with the court, (ii) court **hearings** being scheduled, (iii) the use of various litigious tools, such as **discovery** and depositions (outside the scope of this book), and (iv) repetitive requests for information and/or documentation.

So then, what can be done when one party does not wish to go through with a divorce? Unfortunately, there are not many options here. However, one option is to try to impress upon the defender the fact that the divorce will almost certainly be granted if only one party wants a divorce (see the section titled *"Grounds for a Divorce"* earlier in this chapter). Asking the defender to consult with an attorney to learn about divorce grounds and the meaning of irreconcilable differences may be just the ticket to open up the defender's mind to **non-adversarial** (i.e., out-of-court) resolution. The message to send to the defender is: "If the divorce will most definitely be granted, then why make the divorce process any more difficult or expensive than what it needs to be?"

If the defender finally accepts that the divorce will occur (at least from a legal standpoint), then the defender really only has a couple of choices: (1) either proceed in an amicable fashion in an attempt to minimize the emotional and financial impact on all involved, including any children, or (2) be intentional uncooperative, which may irreparably and emotionally injure those involved, and almost surely increases the time and costs of the case. If both parties are willing to proceed in an amicable fashion, then a non-adversarial method of resolution (i.e., out-of-court) may be a great way to approach your divorce, which is the focus of this book. Non-adversarial methods of resolution will be discussed in detail in later chapters.

Another option for the defender is counseling, if that person is open to counseling. Unfortunately, many people are not willing to meeting with a mental health professional due to feelings of inadequacy, lack of confidence or trust in counseling as a therapeutic tool, fear of losing control, or pride. For example, some people may feel that there is nothing "wrong" with them and, therefore, do not need to see a "shrink." Please note that I hold a very high regard for mental health professionals, and their services are largely underutilized in family law actions. If there are serious emotional issues, a mental health professional can provide invaluable assistance.

The counseling referred to in this section of the book is not *marital* therapy, which focuses on *repairing* a marriage. Instead, the therapy is focused on *separation* and/or assisting with communication. There may be emotional blocks that are preventing a person from accepting that the marriage is over. Alternatively, perhaps there is something that is preventing a person from moving on with his/her life that needs to be resolved. A mental health professional can assist with these sensitive emotional issues, which diffuses negativity. With the reduction or removal of negative emotions, the parties can approach their case from a more logical perspective.

Further still, a mental health professional may be able to teach someone essential communication skills in order to make speaking with the other party more productive. Productive communication will likely make the divorce process (or any other family law matter) more efficient and, therefore, less costly and less time consuming.

While emotional challenges may have no legal relevance, diffusing negative emotions can allow for more thought, focus, concentration, and cooperation. For example, consider infidelity. As mentioned in the section "*Grounds for a Divorce*" mentioned earlier in this chapter, infidelity has no legal significance for **irreconcilable differences** since California is a no-fault state. However, if *emotional* blocks can be diffused, this may help the person to have closure and, therefore, be able to move forward with the divorce more cooperatively, and with a sense of genuine acceptance.

CHAPTER TWO: FEES, EXPENSES AND COSTS

One of the most common questions asked to a family law attorney or mediator is "How much will this cost?" Assuming a **flat fee** is not used, there is no way to gauge the ultimate cost of a family law case. It is not common for flat fees to be utilized in family law cases. There are, however, factors that can be analyzed by the parties that will give some clues as to whether there is a long expensive road ahead. However, before we can even explore the factors that influence cost, we need to define costs. In this book, the term "costs" consists of both fees and expenses. So, let's first explore fees and expenses in more detail.

Fees

Fees are payments made to an attorney or other professional, such as a mediator, to help you with your case. If an attorney is hired, the most common fees in a family law case are legal fees.

While there are several different pay structures offered by attorneys, family law attorneys typically have a **retainer** that is billed against periodically for work that was done in the case. Therefore, the saying "time is money" truly applies when an attorney or any other professional that bills for time is hired. In other words, the more *time* the attorney or other billed-for-time professional puts into a case, the more the client will be billed pursuant to the professional's hourly rate.

Expenses

Expenses include things such as court filing fees, **process server** fees, **court runner** fees, copy fees, **subpoena** fees, report fees and expert fees. They are case costs that are in addition to fees.

Many of the expenses associated with a family law case depend on the wishes of the parties. For example, if someone wants to have a house appraised, there will be a fee for the appraisal and the report, as well as for any testimony provided by the expert that provided this information and documentation. If subpoenas are issued, this will add to the expenses of the case. If motions are filed with the court, there are filing fees that need to be paid to the court. If someone chooses to hire a person to **serve** papers on the other party, there is an expense for this as well. The list goes on.

Some expenses can be avoided because they do not apply, such as not needing a real estate appraisal if the parties are simply renting and do not own any real property. Other expenses are optional, where a decision will need to be made as to whether to incur such expenses. For example, if the parties do own real property, either party can decide to obtain a professional appraisal, thereby incurring that expense. Other expenses may not be avoided, such as the court filing fee when initiating a divorce proceeding. To the extent that you have a choice as to whether to incur certain expenses, you will need to weigh the amount of the expense against the potential benefit that could be gained in order to make a prudent decision.

TIP: Particularly with non-adversarial (i.e., out-of-court) resolution, in situations where using an expert is prudent, the use of a joint expert should be strongly considered. A **joint expert** is an expert that is hired by both parties and is typically paid for equally by both parties. Having a joint expert, as opposed to each party having hired his or her own expert, not only provides the opportunity to decrease expert expenses, but it also avoids "dueling" expert opinions, which may only exacerbate expenses in the case. You will learn more about joint experts later in this book.

Costs

Unless otherwise indicated, the term "**cost**" as used in this book will include *both* fees and expenses. Now that fees and expenses have been explored, let's return to the question at hand: "How much will my case cost?"

If a paid-for-time professional is involved, such as an attorney, focusing on determining how much *time* the case is expected to take will help you assess cost. It would be misdirected to simply look at, for example, the attorney or mediator's hourly rate without looking at anything else in your case that may influence time.

If time directly impacts how much a case will cost, this leads to the crux of the problem in being able to determine an ultimate cost for a case: *There are factors that are almost entirely out of any professional's control that influence the total cost of a case.* Interestingly, the primary factors that influence the amount of *time* a case will take are within your and the other party's control! The main factors that influence total cost are: (i) Complexity of the case, (ii) cooperation of the parties, and (iii) approach style of the parties. The next chapter will discuss these factors in detail.

CHAPTER THREE: FACTORS THAT INFLUENCE COST

The main factors that influence total cost are: (i) Complexity of the case, (ii) cooperation of the parties, and (iii) approach style of the parties. So then, let's take a look at these factors in more detail.

Complexity of the Case

The more complex the case, the costlier the case will likely be, due to increased time and increased expenses. For example, there is a good chance that a family law case *without* children will take less time than a case with children. There are additional issues to resolve in a divorce case where there are minor children, including custody designations and devising a parenting plan. Further still, a case involving one parent wanting to relocate to a distant county or another state is likely going to have more bumps in the road than a case where the parents live a block away from each other. A case involving multiple pieces of real estate is likely going to take longer than a case with only one apartment being rented as a residence by the two parties. A case involving self-employed individuals almost certainly causes more issues and more analysis versus a case where both parties are W-2 employees. And so forth.

TIP: In financially complex cases, it may be prudent to have a financial expert involved. A financial expert can be a great addition to the legal team. The financial expert can perform things such as (i) analyze the marital standard of living or the marital lifestyle, (ii) analyze cash flow, (iii) calculate net spendable income, (iv) conduct a business valuation, and (v) conduct bank statement reviews. Additionally, a financial expert's opinion is going to be highly regarded and certainly afforded much more credibility than an opinion of a layperson. Finally, a financial expert's fees are generally lower than an attorney's fees, which means that there is a chance that expenditure of fees can be mitigated by having a financial expert handle some of the tasks that an attorney may normally perform, such as bank account analysis and summarization.

Cooperation of the Parties

How well the parties can cooperate and communicate with each other has a direct impact on how complicated the case will be and, therefore, how long the case will take and how much the case will cost. Simply stated, the more the parties can cooperate and communicate with each other, the more likely the case will finish more quickly, and with less cost. On the other hand, the less the parties can cooperate and communicate with each other, the more likely the case will take much longer to finalize, and the more expensive the case will become. There are a few concepts that relate to cooperation between two parties that are helpful to understand: (i) Negative conditioning, (ii) **preliminary settlement thoughts**, and (iii) professionals as conduits. Let's take a deeper look at these concepts now.

Negative Conditioning

Do you remember learning about Pavlov's dogs? The story of Pavlov's dogs was related to the theory of "conditioning" by using dogs as test subjects. For a while, each time the dogs were given their food, a bell was rung. One of the dogs' reactions to being brought their food was salivation. Another reaction was excitement. After some time of performing this pattern of ringing the bell when the food was brought to the dogs, only the bell was rung without bringing any food. The dogs were conditioned to relate the bell being rung to food being provided to them. Thus, the dogs would salivate and immediately become excited just from hearing the bell, even though there was no food. The dogs were conditioned.

Likewise, with people, oftentimes conditioning occurs without even realizing it. With people that are separating, most of the time negative conditioning has occurred between them without being conscious of it. For example, perhaps in the beginning of the deterioration of their relationship, there is some arguing and disagreement. Maybe the disagreement is about how to parent the children of the relationship, or maybe it is how money should be spent or saved. As time moves forward, there is increased disagreement and negativity felt towards the other party. Pretty soon, the parties are conditioned to feel bad when they are simply in each other's presence, when they look at each other, or just by even *thinking* about the other party. In other words, the parties begin to feel upset at each other without uttering a single word!

Indeed, a married person may simply be speaking to someone about his or her spouse while becoming angry and then comment, "I'm sorry, it's just that he/she makes me *so* angry." Another tell-tale sign that negative conditioning has occurred is when you hear someone say "we fight about *everything*."

When negative emotions are present, it is difficult, if not impossible, for some people to think and behave logically, or with any degree of appropriateness. Unfortunately, this behavior can result in separating parents using the children as tools in an attempt to "get back" at the other party, which ultimately hurts the children the most. This type of behavior can irreparably damage the parent/child relationship, as well as negatively impact a child's development. There are also the rare and very unfortunate cases where death results from an angry parent acting against the other parent and/or the children.

If the pattern of negative conditioning is not broken, this certainly contributes to the breakdown of a relationship. Negative conditioning can also continue to cause problems even *after* the parties have separated. For example, co-parenting may be a continuous challenge if the negative conditioning left over from a dissolved relationship cannot be overcome. Discussing relatively simple things such as their child's homework can be challenging if the parties immediately become upset with each other due to continued negative conditioning. In such cases, co-parenting classes may help improve communication between the parties, although individual counseling as an additional tool should also be considered.

For separating individuals, negative conditioning towards each other oftentimes leads to something I refer to as "**reactive devaluation**," which is a result of negative conditioning. Reactive devaluation is when something said by the other party is automatically and immediately shunned or minimized *just because* it came out of the other party's mouth! Yet, had the same thing been said by another person, it would have been respectfully received.

Reactive devaluation is a serious issue that essentially destroys any potential productive communication that could help resolve family law issues, and it certainly negatively impacts the ability of parents to co-parent any of the minor children after they have separated. If reactive devaluation is suspected to be present, the parties should strongly consider therapeutic intervention to break the pattern and to learn non-defensive communication skills. Treatment for reactive devaluation and any negative conditioning should be done as early as possible.

Preliminary Settlement Thoughts

Another example of how the parties' lack of communication can add to increased costs is the inability to come up with preliminary settlement thoughts. By **"preliminary settlement thoughts,"** I mean ideas for potential settlement—not firm agreements—that the parties discuss *without* professionals present. These are thoughts that *may* resolve issues currently under dispute. Those ideas are then brought to the professionals involved, such as attorneys or a mediator, to determine whether any of those ideas will become agreements that will be filed with the court.

Let's say the parties are facing multiple issues. In litigation, if the parties do not discuss anything with each other and attorneys are involved, then the responsibility for settling the case, communications and trial preparation falls entirely on the attorneys (see *"Professionals as Conduits,"* below, to see how this gets expensive quickly). In mediation, if the parties do not discuss preliminary settlement thoughts, then all settlement discussions will need to take place during mediation sessions.

On the other hand, if parties speak with each other and come up with preliminary settlement thoughts regarding at least some of the issues, this jump-starts the settlement discussions and typically reduces the amount of time needed to arrive at and formalize agreements, whether your case is in mediation, collaborative law or litigation. More on mediation, collaborative law and litigation will be discussed later in this book.

Professionals as Conduits

It goes without saying that two people getting along will likely get farther faster than two people that can barely even look at each other. Unfortunately, sometimes negative emotions are so high in one or both parties that they are not speaking to each other at all. In these instances, the attorneys for both parties end up becoming conduits, acting as messengers between the parties. If attorneys are not involved, a party brings the case into court and the judge will make decisions after hearing both sides.

In litigation, if attorneys are involved, discussions are oftentimes done via multiple letters going back and forth between the attorneys for relatively minor things, such as who is going to bring the dog to the vet the following week. There are also likely many phone calls and/or emails between the attorneys. Phone calls, emails and letters are billed to the clients, and they all increase attorney fees.

In mediation and collaborative law, if the parties cannot speak productively, or if they feel too uncomfortable being in the same room as each other, it may be best to split the parties into two separate rooms. In mediation, the mediator floats back and forth between the parties. In collaborative law, the attorneys meet with each other and then the attorneys meet with their clients. The approach of splitting the parties into separate rooms is called "**caucusing**." Whether the case is being mediated or whether it is a collaborative law case, more time will likely be required, which increases legal fees.

Approach Style of the Parties

"Approach style" refers to the personality of each party as it relates to making decisions. One end of the spectrum is the "quick and easy," or less-detailed, approach. On the other end of the spectrum is great detail, analysis and investigation. Depending on where *both* parties fall on this spectrum, this can increase or decrease the amount of time a family law case will take.

As an example, let's apply two extreme approach styles to a **parenting plan**. A parenting plan includes provisions as to when minor children will be in the physical custody of each parent. An extreme example of the quick and easy approach to crafting a parenting plan may sound something like this: "Parenting time to each parent as mutually agreed upon by the parties." That's it. The parenting plan is in place. Now, is this a prudent parenting plan that is duly enforceable? Most of the time the answer is "no." This parenting plan arrangement would not work efficiently for most of the separating parents out there. However, it does save costs up front since it will not take much time to negotiate this plan and to put it in writing. Less time when a professional is involved means less fees that will be billed.

An example of a parenting plan on the detailed end of the spectrum may involve defining, down to the hour, the days and times that each parent would have physical custody of the minor children. Additionally, there may be a holiday plan that specifically defines each holiday, again, down to the hours of exchange. Perhaps "Christmas" is defined as "Christmas Eve at 6:00pm through Christmas day at noon."

Regarding **property** division, a quick and easy example involving two couches is that each party receives one of the two couches of the marriage without valuing the couches to see who ends up receiving more value than the other. As an example of the detailed approach, the couches could be valued with any disparity settled by an **equalization payment** made by the party receiving the couch that is valued higher. In California, an equalization payment is used to ensure that the division of community property between two spouses is equal. If you reside outside California, community property may not apply to you; consult an attorney to be sure.

Here is an example to show you how an equalization payment is calculated: Let's say Wife receives the pink couch worth $1,000 and Husband receives the blue couch worth $500. In this example, Wife would owe Husband $250 to "equalize" the division of community property.

With a less-detailed approach, oftentimes there is less work up front. Less work oftentimes means less time spent investigating and preparing. If an attorney is involved, this oftentimes translates into lower fees since an attorney typically bills for time. However, there could be enforceability issues with this approach (outside the scope of this book). On the other hand, if one or both parties are more detail-oriented, there will necessarily need to be more time spent conducting investigation, analysis and preparation. In this instance, if an attorney is involved, this will likely increase fees up front, but may save on fees that would be incurred down the line if an order needs to be enforced. Being more detailed generally means more accuracy and more enforceability (consult with an attorney regarding enforceability issues). Therefore, the approach style of the parties will influence how long it takes to resolve a case and, consequently, how much the case will cost.

CHAPTER FOUR: RESOLUTION CATEGORIES

This book will focus on explaining three options for working through a divorce or other family law issue. All three options involve the assistance of a family law attorney: (i) **Mediation**, (ii) **collaborative law** and (iii) **litigation**. However, before we can explore the *methods* of resolution, it is important to first understand the *categories* that these methods fall into. Specifically, these categories are (i) **non-adversarial** resolution and (ii) **adversarial** resolution.

Non-adversarial resolution is where the parties to a dispute have a formal written agreement in place stating that they will not bring their case before a judge, nor will they implement various tools commonly found in litigation. Non-adversarial resolution, therefore, could also be called "out-of-court" resolution. The formal agreement usually contains provisions that reflect the parties' willingness to resolve their issues respectfully and in good faith.

A non-adversarial form of resolution is completely voluntary and requires the agreement of the parties to proceed. You cannot be forced to enter into family law mediation or collaborative law, and you cannot be forced to *stay* in a non-adversarial process once it has begun. As such, if the parties cannot resolve any aspect of their **matter**, either party can terminate the non-adversarial process and take their case to court. The resolution methods of *mediation* and *collaborative law* fall under the non-adversarial category.

With *adversarial* resolution, the parties do not have a formal written agreement to stay out of court. Each party is free to seek assistance from a judge at any time, and there are no procedural restrictions agreed upon by the parties. Nonetheless, the parties typically can still attempt to resolve the issues they are facing out of court. If a party wishes to involve the court, a **hearing** will need to be requested or the case is set for trial. When in court, a judge will ultimately make decisions in the form of an order or judgment. The resolution method of *litigation* falls under the adversarial category.

CHAPTER FIVE: CHOOSING A RESOLUTION CATEGORY

How do you know whether a non-adversarial method of resolution may be a good choice for you as opposed to litigating your case? The following are several factors to consider to help you decide.

How Much Control Do You Want Over The Outcome?

In California, family law trials are bench trials, unlike criminal and civil law trials, which are typically tried by jury. A **bench trial** is when the judge wears two hats: one as a judge, the other as the jury, sometimes called the "**trier of fact**." There is no jury since the judge assumes the role as the jury.

Broken down further, this means that, in a bench trial, a judge must apply the law to the admissible facts that are presented to the court. Therefore, it is the responsibility of the parties, or their attorneys if applicable, to provide the court with relevant and admissible facts. Once this is done, the judge will apply the law to those facts and make decisions, which will be in the form of an order or a judgment.

The judge's process can be expressed in a mathematical formula, which I call the **court formula**: Law + Facts = Order or Judgment.

One potential advantage in a non-adversarial form of resolution is that there is no judge involved to apply the court formula. In fact, with relatively few exceptions, the parties have a large degree of flexibility to craft agreements that *deviate* from the court formula! In other words, parties have the opportunity to agree to something *different* then what they would have likely received in court.

Oftentimes, *both* parties leave court feeling dissatisfied with the judge's decisions. This is a "lose/lose" scenario. On the other hand, when the parties *agree* on the outcome—an outcome that they crafted themselves—both parties are happy. This is a "win/win" scenario. The flexibility to deviate from the court formula when the parties choose to keep their case out of court and to work cooperatively is powerful indeed.

I had heard a touching story relayed by a judge that illustrates how important it is for the parties to control the outcome of their case, particularly when there are minor children involved: A mother and a father were divorcing. They could barely speak with each other. Negative emotions were very high and co-parenting was challenging between these parties, to say the least. One day, the parties had a court hearing. At this hearing, the judge was presented with the difficult task of deciding the time the children would spend with each parent since the parties could not agree. The judge paused for a moment, looked down at the parties' legal paperwork on his bench, and then looked up at the parties. In a sincere voice, he said to the parties softly: "I don't even know the color of your children's eyes. Yet, you want *me* to decide when your children get to see each of you?"

The parties know their case and their children more than anyone…more than the attorneys, the court staff and the judge. If parties can put aside their differences to resolve sensitive issues such as custody and parenting time, they have a great opportunity to arrive at terms and conditions that they *both* feel is best not only for themselves, but also for their children. When both parties are happy with the result, the chance of heading back to court anytime soon is not as likely as when one or both parties are angry with the judge's decision.

Do You Want To Avoid Going To Court?

Most family law court hearings are done in a public forum, meaning that the courtroom is open to the public and anyone may listen to the proceedings. It goes without saying that family law proceedings will often contain sensitive information that people feel should remain private. Depending on the location of the courthouse, the courtrooms could be packed with people that are listening to the sensitive facts of your case and the judge's ruling. Large cities tend to have more people in the court audience.

Standing in front of a judge in a room full of strangers can also be downright nerve-racking. When you are extremely nervous, it is much more difficult to think and speak. You may forget to get a critical point across to the judge. Alternatively, maybe the point was made, but it was communicated poorly and misunderstood as a result.

On the other hand, in non-adversarial resolution, most of the time the judge is not directly involved. Instead, there are a series of out-of-court meetings to resolve all of the issues in the comfort of an office or a conference room without any strangers looking on or listening to the negotiations. Thus, articulation of thoughts tends to be easier and more relaxed. Parties can focus on positive resolution in a comfortable, safe and private environment.

Can You And The Other Party Cooperate?

Another factor to consider is the level of cooperation and communication you have with the other party. Some parties cannot look at each other, let alone speak to each other, and they are not willing to work on their communication. In non-adversarial resolution, there are a series of out-of-court meetings where the issues of the divorce or other family law case are discussed, including child custody, spousal support and **property** division. While there should be no expectation that you and the other party will smoothly work out every issue, there should be some degree of ability for you and the other party to communicate respectfully.

Some turbulence is expected during any family law action, which is why attorneys are often involved to assist in a non-adversarial form of resolution. Perhaps therapists are also assisting. The more you and the other party can communicate respectfully, the more likely a non-adversarial form of resolution will be successful.

How Much Do You Trust The Other Party?

When people are divorcing, normal feelings of self-preservation take over. Common questions asked are: What can I do to protect myself? How can I preserve my assets? How can I have enough cash flow to pay my bills and have a decent quality of life? What can I do to make sure I can see my children frequently?

For other family law actions, there are similar questions. These questions are largely built upon fear, including a feeling of lack of control. As a result, there tends to also be feelings of mistrust in the other person. These feelings are completely natural and normal. Therefore, it would be unrealistic to say that you need to *completely* trust the other person for a non-adversarial form of resolution to work. However, if there is utter and complete distrust in the other person, then a non-adversarial form of resolution is less likely to be successful.

Let's say the other party has hidden assets throughout the marriage, has a criminal record of fraud and has a history of lying. While this is a strong example, it is meant to display the type of conduct that would likely cause the other party to experience a complete loss of trust, and rightfully so. When there is little or no trust, agreements will almost surely take longer to reach, if reached at all. This is because statements made in meetings will not likely be trusted, which will typically require additional information or documentation to prove that what is being said is true.

For example, let's say a party indicates that he/she earns $50,000 per year. When there is a high level of distrust, pay stubs may need to be provided to prove that the income is, in fact, $50,000 per year. On the other hand, if there is a fairly high level of trust between the parties, it may be agreed that pay stubs are not required to prove the stated income.

If there are serious concerns over trust, then non-adversarial resolution may not work, at least as quickly as if there was some level of trust. On the other hand, if there is a certain amount of trust between the parties, then chances are that a non-adversarial resolution will be successful with agreements reached in a timely fashion. In fact, with the right help from a mediator or attorney, additional trust could actually be gained in a non-adversarial form of resolution.

Has There Been Any Domestic Violence?

If there has been domestic violence between you and the other party, it is very possible that the victim will not feel comfortable speaking to, or being in the presence of, the perpetrator. When there is a history of domestic violence, the chances are less that a non-adversarial process will be successful. What's more, if there is a domestic violence restraining order ("DVRO") in place, a non-adversarial process may be inadvisable since DRVO's almost always include a "stay-away order" where the restrained party must stay a certain physical distance away from the victim, such as "100 yards." A physical get-together within the stay-away order's parameters is a *violation of the order*. **Litigation** may make the most sense, or it may be the only viable option.

TIP: The advancement of technology may be an option to allow the parties to meet out of court in a non-adversarial process *without* violating a domestic violence restraining order that only contains a stay-away order. **Web meetings** are when parties meet in a virtual meeting space over the internet where they can still see and hear each other and also review documents!

Note, however, that some domestic violence restraining orders also contain a "no-contact" order. A no-contact order may state that the parties cannot communicate with each other at all or only regarding certain topics, such as co-parenting, regardless of the medium used. If this is the case, then a web meeting will violate this order unless the order is modified to specifically allow such communications. If there is a DVRO in place and you are considering a non-adversarial mode of resolution, you should definitely speak to an attorney before getting started.

Do Both Parties Want A Divorce?

If the action is a divorce, do both parties want to divorce, or does only one party want to divorce? If only one party wants to divorce, then an assessment should be made on the party that does *not* want the divorce as to whether this person accepts the divorce occurring and respects the other party's decision to obtain a divorce. If there is acceptance, then there is more of a chance a non-adversarial process will be successful.

On the other hand, if there is not acceptance of the divorce, there is less of a chance a non-adversarial process will be successful. In such a case, there could be an ulterior motive in entering into a non-adversarial process. For example, there may be a belief that the other person could be "won" back if given the chance to speak to the other party during mediation or collaborative law. This behavior will likely cause major problems in an out-of-court method of resolution since much time and money will be spent in trying to get assistance in separating, which will likely fail when the parties fail to reconcile. At this point, the parties will likely end up going to court, in effect paying twice—once for the non-adversarial case, and then again in the litigation case.

Common actions taken by someone trying to win back the affection of another party include the following: (i) Taking steps to stall the case, which causes a delay in the case moving forward with resolution; (ii) purposely taking steps to retaliate against the other party, such as not fully disclosing assets; and (iii) emotional difficulties.

The bottom line: If you suspect that the other person does not want to divorce and you do, you should ask yourself whether you believe the other person will proceed through non-adversarial resolution in good faith, and whether you believe the other person respects and accepts your decision to divorce.

Can The Children's Needs Be Placed First?

Some separating parents can put their children's needs before their own needs, recognizing the importance that each parent plays in their children's lives. Of course, this assumes that both parents make decisions in the children's best interests. In other words, while there might be a difference in parenting style, it is not something that causes concern regarding the children's health, safety and welfare. There is a belief that the other parent can adequately care for the children when that parent has physical custody of them. These cases may work out very well in a non-adversarial form of resolution.

On the other hand, unfortunately, some parents inappropriately use their children as tools to hurt the other party...to "get back" at the other party. For example, maybe a parent wants more time with the children only to increase or decrease child support. Alternatively, maybe a parent is attempting to alienate the children from the other parent by speaking harshly about the other parent to the children. Maybe one parent knows how much it would hurt the other parent to lose time with the children and, therefore, purposely attempts to reduce parenting time to the other parent with the sole purpose of hurting that parent. These types of cases are less likely to be successful in non-adversarial resolution, unless this behavior can be corrected.

What Is Everyone's State of Mind?

The following is a great question to be able to test a state of mind that is helpful to a non-adversarial form of resolution: "How can I—within reason and without sacrificing my own values—alleviate the *other party's* concerns?" The ability to be able to genuinely ask this question reconciles a desire for self-protection and, at the same time, retains integrity. It also tests each party's willingness to try to see the other person's perspective and, at the same time, focus on a "win/win" resolution. If you *and* the other party are willing and able to genuinely ask yourselves this question, you are well on your way to being able to enter into a non-adversarial form of resolution. If not, then litigation may be the best choice.

Which Is Cheaper...Adversarial Or Non-Adversarial Resolution?

We have explored many factors to help you determine whether out of court resolution may be a good choice for your case, including cooperation, communication and state of mind...but what about cost? For example, is it cheaper to mediate a case instead of litigating a case?

Since the primary influence of cost lies with the parties, it is unknown which category of resolution will be the cheapest or most efficient (see the chapter titled *"How Much Will My Case Cost?"* for a detailed explanation of why cost is largely in the hands of the parties). However, I can provide examples of costs that are often associated with each of the three forms of resolution that have been referenced in this book (i.e., **litigation**, **collaborative law** and **mediation**) so you can be aware of what to expect and to help you choose a category that feels most comfortable for you. Let's look at the following costs and influences of cost: (i) Attorneys, (ii) experts, (iii) time, and (iv) formal discovery.

Attorneys

In litigation, despite a popular misconception otherwise, attorneys are *not* required. Oftentimes people hire attorneys for peace of mind. Specifically, attorneys do the following: (i) They help take the fear out of the unknown; (ii) they ensure that documentation is completed correctly; (iii) they ensure that legal documentation is timely and appropriately filed with the court and **served** on the other party; (iv) they will appear in court with you and speak to the judge on your behalf; (v) they protect your interests; and (vi) they know how to make sense of all the various and complex family laws. Of course, attorneys typically come at a steep price. If *both* parties each hire their own attorney, the total fees paid to the attorneys in litigation can easily be in the tens of thousands of dollars.

In litigation, any outstanding issues that cannot be resolved through out-of-court settlement will be brought before a judge for decision at a trial or a **hearing**. Attorney fees to prepare for and attend trial can be enormous, easily reaching to tens of thousands of dollars. The more complex the case is, the more the trial process will likely cost.

In collaborative law, while each party is required to have his or her own attorney, there are no court appearances, unlike litigation where court appearances are commonplace.

In mediation, parties are *not* required to hire their own **consulting attorney**. Instead, the only required professional is the mediator, who is typically a family law attorney. With mediation, both parties hire *one* attorney who sits as the mediator. Similar to collaborative law, the mediator does not attend any court appearances. With litigation, each party *may* hire his/her own attorney. With collaborative law, each party *must* hire his or her own attorney. With mediation, each party *may* hire his or her own consulting attorney.

With both mediation and collaborative law, assuming the case resolves in a settlement, there are no hearings, other than potential status hearings where the court checks in to see where your case stands. Again, assuming a settlement, no trial would be scheduled.

Trial and Long-Cause Hearing Costs

If you are in the adversarial category, your case can be set for a trial or **long-cause hearing**. If you are in the non-adversarial category, your case decisions are not placed in front of a judge. Therefore, there are no trial or long-cause hearing costs associated with non-adversarial resolution, assuming it is successful.

Trial and long-cause hearing costs are very expensive. For example, if experts are involved, they typically charge their own **retainers** and hourly fees for trial preparation and testimony. Additionally, when one party hires an expert, the other party oftentimes follows suit by hiring his/her own expert.

The attorney also spends an incredible amount of time preparing for and conducting a trial or long-cause hearing.

Another possible trial cost is having to hire a court reporter if the court does not provide a complimentary reporter.

Appeal

There could be additional costs beyond a trial, including, but not limited to, appeal actions that are very expensive. On the other hand, in non-adversarial resolution, assuming there is a global resolution of all issues, there typically is no trial or appeal. In fact, the right to a trial or an appeal could be waived as part of the settlement terms. In non-adversarial resolution, there is a settlement agreement that relays all of the terms and conditions agreed to by the parties, which is then filed with the court for approval. Therefore, there is no contested issue to appeal.

Experts

While not required, oftentimes there are experts in litigation cases, including, but not limited to, business valuators, real estate appraisers and financial experts. Typically, when each party hires an expert, the experts each come back with opinions that favor his/her own client. When this occurs, it is common for parties to be even more entrenched in their positions. Accordingly, trials are often scheduled when experts are involved—typically at very high rates.

In a non-adversarial mode of resolution, if it is prudent to involve an expert, oftentimes both parties hire and share the costs of one expert, called a **joint expert**. A joint expert is neutral and does not advocate for either party. The hiring of a joint expert avoids dueling opinions because there is only one opinion being given by a single expert who is working for both parties. While a joint expert may be hired in litigation, this oftentimes does not occur because of the adversarial nature of litigation.

Regardless of the method of resolution, hiring a joint expert is typically cheaper than each party hiring his or her own expert. This being said, there is a greater chance a joint expert will be agreed upon in non-adversarial resolution versus litigation. If attorneys are involved in litigation, the attorney will assist with the selection of an expert.

Time to Resolve the Case

As far as time for a case to resolve, this varies case by case. However, it is not uncommon for litigation cases to carry on for years. Oftentimes this is due to the parties' lack of cooperation. If attorneys are involved, more time likely also means more billable hours. If parties are cooperating for the most part, there is a good chance the issues will be resolved quicker, thereby reducing the overall amount of time for the case to come to an end. What's more, if the parties' attorneys have a good rapport with one another, there is a better chance the case will resolve quicker.

The degree of cooperation between the attorneys and other team members in collaborative law plays a role in how long the case will take. The more the professionals cooperate, the quicker the case will likely go. Therefore, feel free to ask whether the professionals involved have a good rapport with one another.

In my experience, mediation cases tend to be quicker and less expensive than litigation. One reason for this is because there aren't too many "cooks in the kitchen." If the parties do not choose to hire another professional, the mediator and the two parties are the only ones involved. If the mediator has nailed down an efficient process, a case can be resolved relatively quickly, and the parties typically share the mediator's fees. In litigation, the parties typically pay all the costs of their own attorneys.

Formal Discovery

In litigation, it is common for parties to engage in formal requests for information and documentation, called **discovery**. The purpose and various types of discovery are beyond the scope of this book, but discovery is mentioned since it tends to be very expensive and can easily cost hundreds, if not thousands, of dollars. Typically, there is no formal discovery in a non-adversarial mode of resolution. In fact, the non-adversarial agreement signed by the parties may actually prohibit the use of discovery. In such cases, the agreement usually treats the issuance of formal discovery by either party as an automatic termination of the non-adversarial process.

CHAPTER SIX: POTENTIAL BENEFITS OF NON-ADVERSARIAL RESOLUTION

There are potential benefits with the non-adversarial methods of resolution of **mediation** and **collaborative law**. The following are a few.

Avoidance of Hearing and Trial Costs

Court work is expensive, period. If the parties are heading to court for trial or for **hearings**, there are significant preparation and appearance **costs**. If the parties are not going to court, as is the case with non-adversarial forms of resolution, those types of costs can be avoided.

Increased Cooperation

Since most things in a non-adversarial form of resolution are done by agreement, including the first agreement of entering into a non-adversarial form of resolution, there tends to be more cooperation between the parties right from the get-go. Cooperation between the parties tends to decrease the amount of time a case will take, which, in turn, tends to minimize costs.

The Hiring Of Joint Experts

If experts are involved in a non-adversarial form of resolution, such as a real estate appraiser, it is more likely that the parties will agree to hire a **joint expert** as opposed to each party hiring his or her own "dueling" expert. It is common for two experts to come up with two different opinions. Receiving dueling opinions can create more adversity and increase costs.

On the other hand, having one joint expert means that the expert is neutral and not biased toward either party. Instead, a joint expert is hired by both parties and arrives at results that are not being challenged by another expert, assuming another expert is not later hired. The hiring of a joint expert typically means that both parties are sharing this one expert's fees, as opposed to each paying the entire amount for his/her own expert. Additionally, since there typically is not a challenged opinion provided by another expert, there is not usually an argument over whether the expert's results are accurate, which means reduced costs by avoiding argument between two experts' different opinions.

Mediation: Hiring Only One Professional

In collaborative law, both parties each *must* have their own attorney. In litigation, although not required, each party often ends up hiring an attorney for representation at court appearances, to draft documents, to conduct research, etc. In mediation, the hiring of a consulting attorney is optional, and many times the parties do not end up hiring their own attorney.

There are pros and cons to having and not having an attorney involved during mediation (see the chapter titled *"Mediation"* for more information on consulting attorneys). It is quite possible that the only professional involved in mediation is the mediator, which is typically a family law attorney. Therefore, instead of both parties having to pay for their own attorney's fees, the parties can choose to equally share in the mediator's fees and other fees, such as expert fees, court filing fees and court runner fees. A **court runner** is someone who is hired by a mediator or attorney to file documents with the court on your behalf. This sharing of fees is attractive to many people, particularly after learning that it is possible that one of the parties could be ordered to pay the other party's attorney fees!

CHAPTER SEVEN: CONFIDENTIALITY

The term "**confidentiality**" simply means that a writing or oral assertion cannot be made admissible as evidence for consideration by a judge, nor can the writing or oral statement be communicated to others. If there is a law or a rule where the parties are afforded confidentiality, the parties will likely feel more comfortable in speaking with each other and other professionals involved in the case since the discussions and writings will remain private. For example, if you have the assurance that a settlement offer you intend to make will not later be used against you in court, then you will feel more comfortable in making the settlement offer. Confidentiality fosters cooperation and promotes settlement.

There is no confidentiality protection that applies to the litigation process, per se, that prevents writings or oral assertions from being admitted into evidence. On the other hand, non-adversarial processes typically have confidentiality protection. However, there is a difference in how confidentiality applies to both mediation and collaborative law in California (if you reside in another state, consult with an attorney for confidentiality laws in your area). Let's see how.

Confidentiality in Collaborative Law

There is no law, per se, that specifically applies confidentiality to a collaborative law case. Nonetheless, there are oftentimes agreements in place that are signed by the parties, their attorneys and other professionals involved in the case that various writings and oral statements will be confidential and inadmissible as evidence. This confidentiality agreement may also become an order of the court if the agreement is filed with the court. In collaborative law, confidentiality is based on the rules of contract law and good faith.

Confidentiality in Mediation

In mediation, on the other hand, there are specific **statutes** (i.e., laws) that automatically provide confidentiality to "mediations" and "mediation consultations," without the parties having to enter into a contract, and without needing an order from the court. California Evidence Code Section 1119 states, in pertinent part:

"(a) No evidence of anything said or any admission made for the purpose of, in the course of, or pursuant to, a mediation or a mediation consultation is admissible or subject to discovery, and disclosure of the evidence shall not be compelled, in any arbitration, administrative adjudication, civil action, or other noncriminal proceeding in which, pursuant to law, testimony can be compelled to be given.

(b) No writing…that is prepared for the purpose of, in the course of, or pursuant to, a mediation or a mediation consultation, is admissible or subject to discovery, and disclosure of the writing shall not be compelled, in any arbitration, administrative adjudication, civil action, or other noncriminal proceeding in which, pursuant to law, testimony can be compelled to be given.

(c) All communications, negotiations, or settlement discussions by and between participants in the course of a mediation or a mediation consultation shall remain confidential."

California Evidence Code Section 1115 defines "mediation" and "mediation consultation":

"(a) 'Mediation' means a process in which a neutral person or persons facilitate communication between the disputants to assist them in reaching a mutually acceptable agreement.

…

(c) 'Mediation consultation' means a communication between a person and a mediator for the purpose of initiating, considering, or reconvening a mediation or retaining the mediator."

Broken down simply, all written communication and oral statements made during a mediation session or a mediation consultation are confidential (i.e., meaning cannot be disclosed) and inadmissible as evidence. Like many laws, there are exceptions; these exceptions to mediation confidentiality are beyond the scope of this book.

The mediation confidentiality also applies to others involved in the mediation process. Evidence Code Section 1115(b) states: "'Mediator' means a neutral person who conducts a mediation. 'Mediator' includes any person designated by a mediator either to assist in the mediation or to communicate with the participants in preparation for a mediation."

This statutory protection affords mediating parties the comfort to be able to speak openly and freely, without fear that something can later be used against them.

CHAPTER EIGHT: RESOLUTION METHODS

We have now discussed the two *categories* of resolution: (i) Adversarial (in-court) and (ii) non-adversarial (out-of-court). We have also discussed various factors to help you determine whether a non-adversarial process may be a good approach for your case. Now it is time to explore the resolution *methods* within those categories: (i) **Litigation** (adversarial category), (ii) **collaborative law** (non-adversarial category) and (iii) **mediation** (non-adversarial category).

In order to make an educated decision as to which resolution method may be comfortable for you, it is important that you understand them. You may ask, "Why do I need to know about the *adversarial* category if I am interested in *non-adversarial* resolution?" Good question.

In order to know where you are going, you need to know where you are starting from. Litigation occurs if the parties do not agree to enter into a non-adversarial form of resolution. In other words, litigation is where you are starting from. In order to understand the differences and the potential benefits of the non-adversarial forms of resolution, it is important to understand what occurs if both parties do *not* agree to handle their divorce or other family law case through a non-adversarial method. So then, let's first discuss litigation.

CHAPTER NINE: LITIGATION

The method of resolution within the adversarial category is **litigation**. In litigation, an attorney is typically not required for a party in a family law proceeding. Even though litigation is in the adversarial category, the parties may actually still try to work out all of the issues amicably *without* judicial intervention. However, in the event they cannot resolve some or all of the issues in their case on their own, the case is placed before a judge by requesting a court **hearing** or setting the case for trial.

At trial or a hearing, it is the judge who decides the case outcome. When a **matter** is brought into court, the judge must apply the law to the parties' facts to make decisions about the case. It is the parties' responsibility to ensure that they submit relevant and admissible evidence to the judge and to argue the law to their facts to have the best chance in receiving a favorable result.

With family law trials in California, there is no jury. Instead, trials in California family law matters are called "**bench trials**," meaning the judge is the only one hearing and ruling on the case. There is no jury. Nonetheless, all of the typical procedural rules still apply, including the rules of evidence, opening and closing statements, direct and cross examination, etc. Family law proceedings are generally open to the public, which means anyone can be present in court and listen to what is said. In family law, it goes without saying that quite a bit of what is said is sensitive and considered private by one or both parties. Nonetheless, if you are in court, the public hears the details of your case, whether you like it or not.

Do I Need An Attorney For Litigation?

Parties may attempt to litigate their case in **pro per**, meaning they are not represented by an attorney. There are facilitators' offices within the California family courts that provide free assistance to parties with the preparation of various family law documents. However, a facilitator's office cannot provide legal advice, nor can they suggest legal strategy. Other states have their own version of facilitators' offices.

Depending on your **jurisdiction** (i.e., the county of the court where your case will be filed), it can be quite a hassle to meet with a facilitator due to the following: Potentially having to pay for parking, parking a distance away from the court house, having to go through security, and dealing with long lines. It is also possible that your jurisdiction may not have an in-person court facilitator due to budget cuts and, instead, the facilitator is only available via the internet.

Although parties can litigate their case on their own, it is always recommended that a family law attorney provides some assistance, whether from consultations here and there or whether an attorney is retained.

Family law cases are complex and the applicable rules and laws are in a constant state of flux. The legal documentation in family law is laden with pitfalls for the unwary. You want to ensure that your rights are protected, including such things as rights with your children, to ensure that you receive your fair share of the community **property**, to protect a retirement account that took years to acquire, etc. One mistake in any one of these areas could not only be financially costly, but emotionally costly as well. In fact, you may end up paying more to repair a damaged case than what it would have cost if it was done right in the first place. Furthermore, you could be subject to sanctions for doing something wrong.

If possible, involve a family law attorney to ensure your case is being handled correctly and efficiently, even if it is just to consult with an attorney here and there. Involve an attorney as early in the case as possible. The following are some examples of the helpful assistance an attorney can bring to the table in litigation.

Court Appearances

Many, if not most, people are uncomfortable appearing and speaking in court. To make matters worse, most of the time family law hearings are open to the public! This means that anyone can come into the courtroom and listen to your **matter**.

Additionally, much of the time, people do not know what to say to the judge. Instead, many people without an attorney get caught up in red herrings…the emotional and irrelevant facts. At a hearing, you only have a limited time to present your case, so every word counts. You need to know how to prioritize your arguments. You need to know how to recognize red herrings in order to avoid them. Knowing and being able to articulate and argue the law is critical in court.

A family law attorney will have a better chance of getting the relevant information to the judge and an attorney will likely feel more comfortable in doing so. Additionally, an attorney will have better access to helpful law, and an attorney can artfully argue the law to your case. After all, they have been trained to do so. Finally, an attorney may have good rapport with your judge, which may prove helpful to your case. You remember the saying: "It's 'who you know, not what you know." This statement is particularly applicable if your case is in a small town where the legal community is a small group.

Legal Research

Attorneys do not know everything there is to know about the law, and they do not always know the answer to a question off the top of their heads. However, an attorney will likely know where to go to get the answer.

Attorneys have access to materials and resources that most people do not likely have in their possession, and attorneys know how to conduct research into various statutory and **case law**. Trying to do this on your own will likely be a very time-consuming and expensive task, and it may be fruitless anyway.

Negotiations

There is a saying: "Sometimes we don't know so much that we don't know what we don't know." Throughout an attorney's career, chances are that the attorney will have learned a good fix for the issues you are facing. In fact, some family law issues are common and tend to present themselves again and again. An attorney may be able to bring such insight into your **matter** and, thus, have an arsenal of potential solutions for your matter that would not have even crossed your mind. This insight is invaluable and is oftentimes only gained through experience.

Filing and Service of Documentation

I cannot think of anyone that looks forward to taking off a half day of work or more to stand in line in the company of many angry people to file legal documentation with the court. Attorneys oftentimes use **court runners** to file documents on behalf of their clients. Alternatively, the attorneys know of other methods to file documents with the court, such as through the mail, via fax or electronic filing. Your time is certainly precious. With an attorney at your side, you avoid having to spend a good chunk of your time filing documents with the court.

Additionally, attorneys use **process servers** to **serve** (i.e., to formally provide) documents to either the opposing attorney or the opposing party, as the case may be. Sometimes a court runner is also a process server. A party to a family law action cannot serve most legal documentation. Therefore, these headaches can likely be easily handled by the attorney at a very reasonable cost. Otherwise, it is you that needs to find someone that meets the legal criteria to serve the documents. Even if you were to find someone to do this, you must ensure that you fill out the legal documents correctly and that you are using the correct documents.

Service Options with an Attorney in Litigation

If an attorney's assistance is used in litigation, there are three services an attorney can provide that will be discussed in this book. The three service options are: (i) Full service, (ii) partial service and (iii) consult-only. Not all attorneys offer these options, so be sure to check with a prospective attorney to see if he or she offers the service that interests you. Additionally, there may be different interpretations or different structures for these options from one attorney to another. Therefore, you should investigate the specifics of these various options with each attorney you interview.

With An Attorney: Full Service

Full service is the whole kit and caboodle. With this service, the lawyer becomes your **attorney of record**, which means that the lawyer actually "represents" you. The full service option places the largest amount of responsibility for the case with the attorney, including court appearances, document drafting, providing legal advice, conducting legal research, and the filing and service of legal documentation.

When legal documents are prepared, it is the attorney's name that goes in the **caption** at the top of the documentation, along with the attorney's contact information and the name of the party whom the attorney represents.

Typically, the full service option requires the largest **retainer** since the attorney expects to spend more time with this type of service versus partial service or consult-only (see the chapter titled "*A Little about Retainers*" for more information on retainers). Most family law litigation attorneys offer the full service option.

With An Attorney: Partial Service

Partial service is when the responsibility for the case is somehow apportioned between the attorney and the client. There are many different ways to divide this responsibility.

One common partial service arrangement is called "ghostwriting and consulting." In this arrangement, the lawyer does not become the client's attorney of record. Instead, the client is still representing himself or herself. As such, it is the client's name that appears on all the legal documentation. However, it is the attorney who is *drafting* the client's legal documentation behind the scenes (i.e., "ghostwriting"). There is a true art to drafting legal documentation in a family law action. Additionally, well-written legal documentation in a family law action is critical, typically providing evidence and legal argument that will be considered by the court for decision-making. In addition to the drafting of legal documentation, the attorney also provides consulting to the client on an as-needed basis.

Document drafting and consulting are the two primary functions typically provided by an attorney in a partial service arrangement. However, there may be additional services included, such as legal research and the filing and service of legal documentation. The client, then, would remain responsible for negotiations with the other party or other party's attorney, and for making court appearances. Trial work may or may not be included. Before signing any fee agreement, you should clearly understand whether trial work is included and, if so, to what extent. In any case, the partial service fee agreement should clearly state the client's responsibilities and the scope of the attorney's services.

Partial service arrangements usually require a **retainer**, but they are not typically as high as full service retainers since the attorney is not taking on as much responsibility. An attorney will not likely spend as much time working on the case with a partial service arrangement as with a full service arrangement. For more information on retainers, see the chapter titled *"A Little about Retainers."*

Partial service is a great option for people that want to keep legal fees down, or for people that want to handle various aspects of the case on their own. You pay as you go.

With An Attorney: Consult-Only

Consult-only is an à la carte service. With consult-only, there is typically no **retainer** necessary because there is no expectation of continued service. Instead, service is limited to each scheduled consultation.

With consult-only, the client schedules a consultation appointment with the attorney on an as-needed basis. During this appointment, the attorney can review documents that you have prepared and provide you with feedback and strategy regarding your case. You should expect that the attorney will need some time to get up to speed in your case, whether this is an initial consultation or a return consultation.

Payment for the consultation could be due prior to the consultation, at the time of the consultation, or immediately after the consultation. Make sure you understand when you are expected to pay for the consultation, and make sure you know the forms of payment that are accepted by the attorney. Some attorneys do not accept checks; other attorneys do not accept credit cards or do not accept certain credit cards, and so on.

Beware of Free Consultations

Some attorneys offer free initial consultations, while other attorneys charge for them either at the full hourly rate or at a discount. Be careful with free consultations in family law! First, think about the saying, "you get what you pay for." It is possible that the attorney may hold back a bit during the consultation since the legal advice will be free. Second, you should consider the attorney's hourly rate. If the hourly rate is exorbitant, the attorney could be offering a free consultation to entice you to retain, knowing that he or she will make up for the free consultation in later billings. It may make more financial sense to pay for an initial consultation—potentially at a discount—with an attorney that has a reasonable hourly rate. This could save you thousands of dollars over the life of a case.

An attorney's hourly rate can make a large difference in cost. For example, an attorney that spends five hours on a case at an hourly rate of $300 per hour will charge you $1,500 (i.e., 5 hours x $300 per hour). An attorney spending the same five hours on a case at an hourly rate of $400 will charge you $2,000 (i.e., 5 hours x $400 per hour). That's a $500 difference for just *five* hours of work!

If you decide to chance a free consultation, be sure to ask what the attorney's normal hourly rate is. You do not want to build good rapport with the attorney during a free consultation, and then later find out that you need to start all over with another attorney because you feel that the attorney you consulted with for free has an hourly rate that is not within your budget.

CHAPTER TEN: NON-ADVERSARIAL RESOLUTION

Similarities Between Mediation and Collaborative Law

The two methods of non-adversarial resolution discussed in this book are **mediation** and **collaborative law**. Any references to "non-adversarial resolution" in this book will, therefore, collectively refer to mediation and collaborative law. This chapter will explain these two methods in greater detail so you can understand their similarities and their differences. Learning about these resolution methods will help you decide which option is the most comfortable for you, if any. First, let's explore their similarities. The differences between mediation and collaborative law will become apparent when you read about mediation and collaborative law in their dedicated chapters later in this book.

Similarity No. 1: Purpose

The first similarity of mediation and collaborative law is their purpose. First and foremost, both methods are designed to keep you out of court. By keeping your case out of court, you and the other party retain full control over the outcome of your case. It is you—not a judge—that arrives at the settlement terms for your family law matter. These settlement terms ultimately become orders of the court, which are then enforceable by a court of law. Other similarities in purpose include: To keep costs down, reduce emotional acrimony, and retain a high amount of confidentiality and privacy.

Similarity No. 2: Process

Another similarity between mediation and collaborative law relates to the process. Both involve a series of out-of-court meetings to discuss and resolve issues. Both involve the assistance of professionals to facilitate agreements. No one can force you to agree.

Similarity No. 3: Voluntary

Both mediation and collaborative law are completely voluntary. No one can force you to choose mediation or collaborative law, and no one can force you to stay in mediation or collaborative law once the process has begun. Mediation and collaborative law can be terminated by either party at any time.

Similarity No. 4: Confidentiality

With both mediation and collaborative law, the negotiations and discussions are typically confidential. This means that discussions cannot be divulged to a court or a third-party unless otherwise agreed. Of course, confidentiality does not apply to the documentation that is prepared and filed with the court. For more information on confidentiality, please see the dedicated chapter on confidentiality found earlier in this book.

Similarity No. 5: Written Agreement

With both mediation and collaborative law, there is a written agreement that is signed by both you and the other party that states you are trying to resolve your case out of court. This agreement typically also contains provisions that state that neither you nor the other party may implement certain tools typically found in litigation. For example, the agreement may state that neither party will file something with the court that results in the calendaring of a court hearing since doing so would go against one of the main purposes of non-adversarial resolution...to stay out of court.

Side Note: When you read the dedicated chapters on mediation and collaborative law, you will actually see some *differences* between mediation and collaborative law regarding some of the items just mentioned. For example, you will see that confidentiality in mediation is applied differently than how confidentiality applies to collaborative law. You will also see that the mediation process differs from the collaborative law process. Rest assured that these concepts will become clearer to you once those respective chapters are explored later in this book.

Bryan C. Ginter, J.D.

Reasons to Consider Non-Adversarial Resolution

With some of the similarities between mediation and collaborative law having been discussed, let's explore some reasons why you may want to consider non-adversarial resolution: (i) Court avoidance, (ii) control over the case outcome, and (iii) opportunity for less time and cost.

Court Avoidance

First, and probably foremost, non-adversarial resolution is meant to keep you out of court to the greatest extent possible. However, there may be scenarios when a court appearance is prudent or necessary. For example, some courts require periodic case status meetings so the court can check in with the parties to see how the case is progressing. Sometimes court hearings are agreed upon by the parties because the hearing is believed to achieve a common goal, such as putting temporary orders in place pending the final settlement. In such an instance, the court appearance is not adversarial in nature.

Many people feel nervous going to court and, at the same time, they feel helpless and scared placing the decisions of their case with a judge. Typically, family law issues are done in open court, meaning the courtroom is open to the public. Many people are uncomfortable in speaking in front of audiences, particularly when they will be speaking about sensitive and private issues. Non-adversarial resolution allows parties to avoid arguing about sensitive issues in a public forum.

Control Over Case Outcome

Another reason to consider a non-adversarial form of resolution is the opportunity for the parties to retain a great degree of control over the outcome of their case, including custody and parenting time, **property** division, and debt assumption. Issues that are against public policy cannot be made into agreements, but these are exceptions to the rule (such a discussion is beyond the scope of this book). Most items agreed upon by the parties will be later approved by the court. For example, how often should the children spend time with you? With the other parent? What assets and debts should you receive? The other party?

A judge may not even know what your children look like. You know your children and your financial circumstances better than a judge or any other professional in your case. With non-adversarial resolution, you and the other party can craft your own outcome…a very powerful benefit to non-adversarial resolution, indeed.

Opportunity for Less Time and Cost

Litigation cases can go on for months or even years. Oftentimes, each party hires his or her own attorney. If experts are involved in litigation, it is common for the parties to have their own experts. If the experts arrive at different conclusions (a common occurrence), it typically fosters more litigation to prove that it is *your* expert that is correct, and that the other party's expert is wrong.

If there are court appearances, it is very expensive for attorneys to both prepare for and attend these appearances. Trial preparation and attendance costs with an attorney can easily reach tens of thousands of dollars. Prior to a trial, many courts require that the parties and their attorneys meet in person at the courthouse to try to resolve their case. This required settlement meeting is called a **mandatory settlement conference**.

With a non-adversarial form of resolution, most, if not all, of the aforementioned litigation processes are avoided. Court is avoided, which means no trial or adversarial court appearances. If experts are involved, typically they are jointly hired and both parties equally share the costs. I once attended a seminar where it was indicated that litigation is, on average, *three times* the cost of mediation. While the accuracy of this statistic cannot be verified, nor can it be guaranteed that mediation or collaborative law will cost less in your case versus litigation, it is my experience, both as a family law litigation attorney and a mediator, that mediation tends to be quicker and less expensive than litigation.

In addition to financial cost, there is also an *emotional* cost to consider. Litigation cases are emotionally exhaustive. It is depleting, on many levels, to constantly fight and be in a state of turmoil. The feeling of fear is typically much greater in litigation versus a non-adversarial resolution method. This is because of the fear of the unknown and loss of control that comes with litigation since it is the judge— not you—who will decide the outcome of your case. It is difficult, if not impossible, to predict what a judge will decide, although a seasoned attorney in a particular locality may have a good sense as to how the judge will rule on certain issues. Nonetheless, the bottom line is that there is no guarantee of a result.

With a non-adversarial form of resolution, the outcome is ultimately the result of agreements between the parties. That, in and of itself, provides comfort...to know that the case is in *your* hands, not a judge's hands. As a result, tension is not typically as high in non-adversarial methods of resolution as it is in litigation.

Due to the foregoing, non-adversarial resolution typically has a lower financial and emotional cost versus litigation.

Series of Meetings

Non-adversarial resolution typically involves the parties attending a series of out-of-court meetings for discussion and negotiation until all of the issues are resolved. Most of the time these out-of-court meetings are held in an attorney's conference room or office. If it is a collaborative law case, it is customary to alternate meetings between both attorneys' offices so that one meeting will be held at Party One's attorney's office, the next at Party Two's attorney's office, back to Party One's attorney's office, and so on.

There should be a comfortable and protected atmosphere that is created to provide a protected space and safe place during these meetings. Both parties should feel comfortable speaking their minds in a non-defensive, respectful manner. The environment provided for non-adversarial resolution meetings should foster honest and sincere open communication, such that both parties can resolve their differences with respect and dignity.

TIP: Nowadays, it is also possible to meet over the internet via **web meetings**. With web meetings, you can see and hear the other meeting attendees and you can review documents together just as if you were meeting in person! With web meetings, parties can avoid expending unnecessary time and gas money on the road. Web meetings are also an excellent solution if two parties are not residing close to the mediator or attorney's office, or if a party has a job that requires extensive travel.

To attend a web meeting, you will need to have a device that can access the internet, such as a desktop computer, a smart phone or a tablet. The device should also have a web camera and microphone so you can see and hear the other attendees. To avoid audio feedback and increase the quality of the audio, you should wear a headset with a microphone.

Not all family law attorneys and mediators offer web meetings. Therefore, if you are interested in web meetings, you should inquire as to whether web meetings is a service that is offered by the prospective attorney or mediator. If web meetings are offered, you should inquire as to the software used by the attorney or mediator to determine how to connect to the web meeting and to ensure you are comfortable with the software.

CHAPTER ELEVEN: CHOOSING A NON-ADVERSARIAL ATTORNEY

There are some attorneys that do not support or believe in mediation or collaborative law as alternatives to litigation. On the other hand, there are attorneys that believe that litigation is never in the best interests of the parties. Then there are attorneys that believe that both adversarial and non-adversarial resolution have their place, depending on the case facts. So, how can you choose the right attorney for your **matter**?

If you are considering an out-of-court method of resolution, you should choose an attorney that believes in non-adversarial resolution, even if that attorney also offers litigation support as a part of his or her law practice. In fact, it may actually be beneficial to hire a non-adversarial attorney that *also* litigates. This is because the attorney may be able to provide insight to a non-adversarial case that could only be acquired in litigation.

For example, let's say you hired a family law attorney to be your mediator, and this attorney also handles litigation cases. This family law attorney mediator could provide an opinion as to how he or she feels your judge may rule on a particular issue if the attorney has appeared in front of that judge before. The attorney would have a feel for the personality of the judge and how that judge tends to rule on various issues due to his or her litigation practice, which could only be gained through experience as a litigation attorney.

Another example may be when the family law attorney mediator is familiar with a judge assigned to your case that routinely grants equal parenting time between two parents, or perhaps there is a local custom in the community where all of the family law judges routinely do not order grandparent visitation. This experience may be invaluable where two parties are at a stand-still regarding a particular issue. In these instances, the attorney mediator can provide feedback that could help facilitate agreements and to move beyond a deadlock.

Be very cautious about the attorney that has the "bulldog litigator" reputation. Also, be wary of an attorney that has never mediated before, but, for your case, the attorney is "willing" to make an exception to mediate your case. There is a paradigm shift that often needs to occur when a litigation-only attorney decides to expand his or her practice to incorporate non-adversarial resolution. The approach to non-adversarial resolution is much different than a litigation approach. It is important that you choose an attorney that already has a good understanding of the non-adversarial process and how it differs from litigation.

Additionally, there are training courses specifically for mediation and collaborative law. If you are considering non-adversarial resolution and you are consulting with various attorneys, whether for mediation or collaborative law, you should find out what specific training the attorney received that relates to the method of resolution you want to use. Perhaps the attorney also has a **curriculum vitae** (i.e., a professional resume) that contains previous training and experience for you to view at a glance.

The following are some great questions you can ask a prospective attorney to help gauge competence for non-adversarial resolution: Have you lectured on mediation or collaborative law? How long have you been practicing family law? Do you only practice family law, or do you also practice other areas of the law? How long have you been practicing mediation/collaborative law? Do you have any publications related to mediation or collaborative law? What professional groups or associations do you belong to relating to mediation/collaborative law?

The more passionate an attorney is about mediation or collaborative law, the more mediation and collaborative law training, publications, etc. you will see in the answers to your questions. You want an attorney that is passionate about non-adversarial resolution. Activities and education related to mediation and collaborative law is a great measure of this passion.

CHAPTER TWELVE:
COLLABORATIVE LAW

Collaborative law is a team-based approach to resolving family law issues out of court. In the California Family Code, it is referred to as "collaborative law process."

Unlike litigation and mediation, each party *must* have his or her own attorney in collaborative law. However, attorneys in collaborative law are more like managers, organizing and supervising the case from start to finish. Of course, as legal representatives of their clients, attorneys ensure that the client is educated, informed and protected throughout the case. Attorneys still owe their clients a duty of loyalty in collaborative law. However, this advocacy is balanced with a tempered approach to the case.

Despite the California requirement that an attorney zealously advocates for his or her client, there is a concept of *transparency* in the process. Transparency means that the lines of communication are open and there is a strong desire that the process remains respectful and that the parties retain their dignity along the way. To a large degree, this means "no secrets." If there is a concern by one of the parties or by one of the team members, it is discussed and worked through so the process is not negatively impacted and so the team can move forward positively.

In addition to attorneys, there may be other professionals involved, such as a child specialist, communication specialist, or financial specialist. This is why collaborative law is referred to as a "team-based" approach.

Authority for Collaborative Law

As of the writing of this book, California Family Code Section 2013 is the only statewide authority for parties to enter into collaborative law as a recognized method of non-adversarial resolution. If you reside in a different state, consult with a family law attorney to learn about the laws applicable to collaborative law in your area. California Family Code Section 2013 states:

"(a) If a *written agreement* is entered into by the parties, the parties may utilize a collaborative law process to resolve any matter governed by this code over which the court is granted jurisdiction pursuant to Section 2000.

(b) 'Collaborative law process' means the process in which the parties and any professionals engaged by the parties to assist them agree *in writing* to use their best efforts and to make a good faith attempt to resolve disputes related to the family law matters as referenced in subdivision (a) on an agreed basis without resorting to adversary judicial intervention" (emphasis added).

Family Code Section 2000, referred to in Family Code Section 2013 states: "This part applies to a proceeding for dissolution of marriage, for **nullity** of marriage, or for **legal separation** of the parties." Once again, a **dissolution of marriage** is a divorce. While this code only lists three types of legal actions that can be resolved with collaborative law, it is this my opinion that collaborative law can be used to resolve *additional* legal issues in family law. For example, collaborative law is a great process for **premarital agreements**, also known as "prenuptial agreements," since it is beneficial and sometimes required for the parties to have their own attorney.

The Collaborative Law Team

As mentioned above, the parties in collaborative law must have their own respective attorney. The collaborative law team consists of (i) the parties, (ii) the attorneys for each party, and (iii) other potentially involved professionals. While there are a series of meetings that occur to resolve all of the issues in the case, it is not necessary for *all* of the team members to be present at every meeting. Oftentimes it is only some of the team that meet to resolve particular issues.

Let's dive a bit further into the collaborative law team so you can better understand their roles. Specifically, you will learn about the attorneys, the mental health professionals and the financial specialists.

Attorneys in Collaborative Law

Unlike litigation or mediation, both parties *must* have an attorney in collaborative law. The attorneys in collaborative law, however, are more like managers of the process, rather than the heavy-hitting advocates people think about when a case is litigated. This is not to say that the attorneys do not protect their clients. Indeed, it is absolutely the attorney's duty to ensure that they are adequately representing and protecting their clients' interests. However, in collaborative law, the attorneys should be representing the parties in a cooperative—rather than adversarial—manner.

In order to choose collaborative law as a non-adversarial method of resolution, the parties and their attorneys must sign an agreement that is filed with the court that states, among other things, that the parties are choosing collaborative law as their method of resolution. There is typically a provision written into the collaborative law agreement that is meant to be an incentive to help keep the parties committed to attaining a successful case. However, since the repercussion of this provision can be quite harsh, it is important that you understand what it is.

Have you ever heard of "motivation by the carrot" and "motivation by the stick"? The "carrot" represents positive motivation. An example of motivation by the carrot is a parent telling a child, "If you clean up your room, I'll give you a cookie." On the other hand, the "stick" represents negative motivation. An example of motivation by the stick is a parent telling a child, "If you don't clean up your room, I will not give you permission to watch television tonight." The incentive that is typically seen in collaborative law contains a motivation by the "stick." Here it is: In the event collaborative law breaks down for any reason, all of the professionals involved in your case, including the attorneys, must be fired. As harsh as this sounds, this provision is intended to keep parties from arbitrarily pulling the plug on the process and, instead, to help focus the parties on continuing positive efforts of resolving their issues. Indeed, the parties will have likely invested quite a bit into the case both financially and emotionally.

Side Note: Due to the many roles an attorney may take in a family law matter, I have created an *Attorney and Therapist Role Chart* to visually and clearly display these roles. The *Attorney and Therapist Role Chart* can be seen in Appendix A of this book.

Mental Health Professionals in Collaborative Law

Mental health professionals are commonly involved in collaborative law as additional team members, although it is not mandatory unless required by the collaborative law group to which your attorneys belong. Refer to the section titled "*Collaborative Groups:*

Is There a Problem Houston?" later in this chapter for more information on collaborative law groups.

There are two roles typically assumed by mental health professionals: (i) Communication specialist and (ii) child specialist. Note that the mental health professional cannot be *both* a communication specialist and a child specialist in the same **matter** since this is a conflict of interest. Let's now explore these two roles in more detail.

Mental Health Professional as Communication Specialist

A communication specialist is a mental health professional that assists the parties with—yes, you guessed it—communication!

Some people refer to communication specialists as "divorce coaches." I feel that the term "divorce coach" causes confusion and, therefore, should not be used. First, the term "divorce coach" implies that this role can only be utilized if the case is a divorce. However, collaborative law process can also be applied to other matters, such as **legal separation, nullity** and **premarital agreements**.

Secondly, the term "divorce coach" sounds like the communications specialist is there to provide guidance, or "coaching," with all aspects of the case. This is not true. The communication specialist is there for one purpose…to aid in communication. Due to the foregoing, the term "communication specialist" will be used to refer to this professional role as discussed in this book.

It is possible to hire one communication specialist for both parties, or for each party to hire his or her own communication specialist. Even though the communication specialist could be a licensed therapist, the communication specialist is not supposed to be providing therapy, per se, to the parties. Instead, the communication specialist assists with diffusing negative emotions and provides tools to assist with non-defensive and productive communications.

It is my belief that one of the primary causes of relationship struggle is defensive communication. Unfortunately, defensive communication has become such a norm for a large part of our society that it typically occurs without any conscious awareness. If there is no awareness of a problem, then there is nothing to fix. A mental health professional sitting as a communication specialist can assist with diffusing defensive communication, and provide tools for productive communication.

Whether there is (i) one communication specialist for *both* parties, (ii) a communication specialist for *each* party, or (iii) no communication specialist for either party largely depends on the group that the collaborative professionals belong to, if any. For more information on how a collaborative law group's guidelines and protocols influence the overall process, see the section titled *"Collaborative Groups: Is There a Problem Houston?"* found later in this chapter.

Mental Health Professional as Child Specialist

A child specialist is a mental health professional that assists if there are any minor children involved in the case. The child specialist is "neutral," meaning that there is only one child specialist per case who is not advocating for either party. Instead, a neutral team member is hired by both parties and assists both parties and the team without any duty of loyalty owed to either party. The child specialist has extensive training with child development.

The child specialist assists primarily in three different ways. Let's explore these ways now.

A Conduit between the Child and the Team

First, the child specialist acts as a conduit between any minor children and the rest of the team, relaying any concerns or wishes of the children. The child specialist may meet with the children and the parents together, with one parent, or with the children alone. Sometimes a child may not be completely forthcoming with one or both parents. Sometimes a child may say something false to a parent without the intent to harm or mislead a parent. For example, each parent may hear conflicting information from their child because the child tells the parents what the child believes *each parent* wants to hear, instead of what the child actually feels.

A good child specialist can win the trust of a child and find out what things are bothering or negatively impacting the child and then relay this sensitive information to the rest of the team. The feedback of a child from the child specialist may take a parent completely by surprise. Perhaps a parent was acting or behaving in such a manner with a child that made the child feel uncomfortable, but the parent had no idea he or she was negatively impacting the child. Such feedback could help enable the parent to incorporate better parenting skills that will foster a more positive relationship with the child.

Child Development Education in General

Second, the child specialist provides education to the rest of the team regarding child development in general, including child development normally seen with children of similar ages to the children that are involved in the case. This information is helpful so the parents and the rest of the team can understand what developmental stage the children are currently in and, thusly, what most influences or impacts the child at that stage. It also helps the parents and the team better prepare for future stages.

Child Development Feedback Regarding Any Minor Children of the Case

Third, the child specialist provides feedback that is specific to the children involved in the case regarding where the children are in their development. Are the children behind where they should be developmentally? Are they advanced? Are they on par?

For example, if the separation of the parents has negatively impacted the children, it is possible that the children have not developed to where they should be in one or more areas of their lives, including, but not limited to, speech and cognitive capabilities. Such information will help the parties and the professionals come together as a team for the common good of the children, to repair any damage from the past, and to determine how to best move forward in the future.

Other Mental Health Professional Roles

Mental health professionals could also assume other roles in a collaborative law case.

First, a mental health professional may be an individual therapist for one or both parties. This may be particularly beneficial where a party is harboring a large amount of negative emotion. Maybe infidelity was involved, or perhaps there was some emotional abuse. Receiving assistance from a mental health professional acting as an individual therapist may be able to provide recovery and closure to such issues, which will help the process move forward more smoothly. It is difficult to think logically when negative emotions are present, such as fear, anger or sadness. Diffusing negative emotions will increase the ability to think with more clarity, which, in turn, will help the parents focus on positive outcomes.

Second, a mental health professional may be a co-parenting counselor. **Co-parenting counseling** is where the parents learn tools to be able to positively communicate with each other regarding the care and upbringing of their children.

Third, a mental health professional could be a **reunification counselor**. If there is any estrangement that has occurred between a parent and a child, a reunification counselor can help rekindle a broken or loose bond between a parent and a child and foster a stronger relationship. For example, let's say one of the parents was in the military and was, therefore, absent a large amount of time. A reunification counselor can assist in connecting the estranged parent and the child.

Side Note: Due to the many roles a therapist may assume in a family law matter, I have created an *Attorney and Therapist Role Chart* to visually and clearly display these roles. The *Attorney and Therapist Role Chart* can be viewed in Appendix A of this book.

Financial Specialists in Collaborative Law

A financial specialist is usually a neutral expert (i.e., an expert assisting both parties) that assists with one or more financial facets of the case. The following are some examples of how a financial specialist can assist in a non-adversarial case:

Disclosure Preparation

In a California divorce or **legal separation**, the parties must disclose all of their (i) assets, (ii) debts, (iii) income and (iv) expenses to each other. There are special forms that are completed by both parties to make such a disclosure. The financial specialist can assist with the preparation of these forms. If you reside outside California, chances are that your state also has some type of financial disclosure requirement where a financial specialist can help. Consult with an attorney to be sure.

Child Support and Spousal Support Calculations

A financial specialist can also assist with determining an acceptable child or spousal support amount to be paid by one party to the other. For example, regarding *spousal* support, the financial specialist can analyze the financial pictures of each party to determine the needs of the *supported* spouse and the ability of the *payor* spouse. Note that the financial expert cannot provide legal advice.

Attorney Fees to be Paid by a Party

A financial specialist can be hired to calculate a potential attorney fee payment by one party to the other. As with spousal support in California, typically an attorney fee payment is based on the needs of the supported spouse and the ability of the payor spouse to pay the fees. Whether or not you reside in California, you should consult with an attorney to determine what laws apply to your case regarding attorney's fees.

Property Division and Equalization Payment

In a divorce or legal separation, an **equalization payment** is a payment provided by one party to the other in order to "equalize" the division of community

property when one party received more in community property value than the other party. A financial specialist can assist in not only determining the value of community property received by both parties, but also in calculating the equalization payment. If you reside outside California, you should consult with an attorney to determine whether you reside in a community property state.

Budgeting

It goes without saying that the financial picture changes drastically when a separating couple goes from, for example, two incomes and *one* set of shared expenses to two incomes with *two* sets of expenses—a set of expenses for each party, such as a house payment. Perhaps one party does not have any income due to the attendance of domestic duties or child rearing.

A financial specialist can prepare a budget and financially plan for both parties to help them adjust to a separate lifestyle. Different scenarios or "what ifs" can also be analyzed, such as selling the family residence versus one of the parties retaining the family residence, or calculating estimates based on various future investments.

Business Characterization and Business Valuation

Maybe one of the parties is self-employed. If so, it may be decided that a business valuation is needed to determine what the community interest or community value is in the business. A financial specialist can help determine what the "character" is of the business. **Characterization** means whether a particular piece of property is one party's separate property, all community property or some combination of separate and community property. If you reside outside California, speak to an attorney to determine how your state's laws apply to property.

If you are considering a financial specialist, you should first determine what type of assistance you are looking for. Is it budgeting? Is it for support calculations? Etc. Then, you should find a financial specialist that has the necessary expertise for the tasks at hand. Not all financial specialists handle all of the tasks mentioned herein, and some financial specialists focus their practice on only one or several of these areas. For example, some financial specialists in the family law community do not perform business valuations.

As with any expert you are considering hiring, it is wise to educate yourself regarding the expert's background, including the expert's education and work experience.

Collaborative Groups: Is There A Problem, Houston?

As of the writing of this book, there are no statutory regulations for collaborative law in California. This means that there are currently no standards or rules for collaborative law professionals.

There are, however, national and local organizations that are self-managed and they have derived *their own* guidelines and procedures for how *they* feel a collaborative law case should be handled. For example, one family law collaborative group may have the requirement that both parties undergo at least one meeting with their own communication specialist.

There is no license or certificate that is given to an attorney to be able to practice collaborative law, and there is no mandatory training for an attorney to practice collaborative law.

A family law collaborative law group may include multiple professionals, including, but not limited to, attorneys, mental health professionals and financial specialists. These groups try to keep business within the group. For example, let's say there is a divorce case and the husband retains a collaborative law attorney in the XYZ Collaborative Group. This attorney will likely provide the husband a pamphlet that includes a list of other attorneys within the same XYZ Collaborative Group. This pamphlet will also likely include the mental health professionals and financial specialists that are also members of the same group. Therefore, if the XYZ Collaborative Group has adopted a requirement that each party must have at least one meeting with a communication specialist, the parties will likely be referred to communication specialists that are also members of the XYZ Collaborative Group.

A collaborative group may have the requirement that only attorneys in the same group may work with each other. This may not be in your best interest. Let's say Husband has an attorney in mind with whom he would like to retain for a collaborative law case, and Wife's attorney belongs to the XYZ Collaborative Group. Husband's attorney is not a member of the XYZ Collaborative Group. The XYZ Collaborative Group has adopted a rule that attorneys in the group may only accept a case if both attorneys are a member of the XYZ Collaborative Group.

The parties now have a dilemma: Does Husband forget about hiring the attorney he wants and, instead, hire an attorney in the XYZ Collaborative Group? Alternatively, does Wife fire her attorney in the XYZ Collaborative Group and, instead, find another attorney? What is really a shame about this scenario is that Husband's attorney could have a fantastic rapport with Wife's attorney, which would likely make for a very cooperative and efficient case, yet the rule in the XYZ Collaborative Group prevents them from helping their clients.

Since each collaborative law group likely has its own self-imposed restrictions, guidelines and protocols that they must follow, you should learn about these guidelines and protocols *before* you retain a collaborative law attorney. To a large degree, these self-imposed guidelines direct the process the case will follow. These guidelines will also set out expectations of each professional involved and the parties. Since everyone in a collaborative case typically signs these guidelines and protocols as a pledge of understanding them and agreeing to follow them, a copy of them should be available upon request.

If you are interviewing an attorney for a collaborative law case, ask whether the attorney belongs to a collaborative group. If so, do yourself a favor and ask for a copy of the group's guidelines and principals so you can make an informed decision as to whether you feel comfortable with those guidelines and protocols. If you do not feel comfortable with a group's policies or procedures, you can simply choose an attorney in a different collaborative group that has policies and procedures that you do feel comfortable with, or, for the ultimate amount of flexibility, you can choose a collaborative law attorney that does not belong to any collaborative law group. A collaborative law attorney that does not belong to any collaborative law group has the flexibility to customize the structure of the collaborative law process to meet each cliénts' particular needs.

As of this writing, it is my opinion that the guidelines and protocols of some collaborative law groups are set up as a "one size fits all" set of rules. In other words, it is believed that the guidelines and protocols should work for *every* case and—to the extent that they do not—it may not be possible to avoid them.

For example, for a group that adopts the requirement that the parties must meet with a communication specialist at least once, this means that the parties have no choice. However, what if the parties do not have the financial resources to do this? Or, what if they simply do not want to meet with a communication specialist? What if parties do not want to have to fire their attorneys if the collaborative case fails? Or, what if one party wants to hire a collaborative attorney that is not a member of a group and the other party hires an attorney in a collaborative group that requires both attorneys belong to the same group?

I believe that the structure of the case needs to be flexible in order to meet the specific needs of each set of clients—not the other way around.

Joining a collaborative group is voluntary and optional for a professional. Choosing an attorney that does not belong to any collaborative group can be good or bad. It can be good if an attorney is a member of a collaborative group since there could be continuing education requirements required by the group to remain a member in good standing. Additionally, being a member of a collaborative group shows a certain sense of loyalty to collaborative law as a non-adversarial method of resolution.

On the other hand, if the attorney is not a member of any group, then the attorney has unlimited flexibility to customize the collaborative law process for each individual case, rather than be bound by a "one size fits all" set of rules and policies that may not necessarily work for your case, or for someone else's case. Additionally, a collaborative law attorney may have undergone collaborative law training even though he or she is not a member of a collaborative law group.

Get educated early in the process before you enter into an agreement with any collaborative law attorney to ensure you will be comfortable with the road that lies ahead.

CHAPTER THIRTEEN: MEDIATION

Family law mediation is another non-adversarial method of resolution that allows people the opportunity to resolve their issues out of court. Let's now discuss mediation in more detail. First, we will look at the legal authority we have in California for mediation, then we will explore the potential professionals involved in mediation.

Authority for Mediation

The authority for mediation is actually not rooted in the California Family Code (if you reside in a different state, consult with a family law attorney in your location to learn about the laws applicable to mediation in your area). Instead, we turn to California Evidence Code Sections 1115 et seq. Evidence Code Section 1115(a) gives us the definition for mediation:

"'Mediation' means a process in which a neutral person or persons facilitate communication between the disputants to assist them in reaching a mutually acceptable agreement."

Evidence Code Section 1115(b) gives us the definition for "mediator":

"'Mediator' means a neutral person who conducts a mediation. 'Mediator' includes any person designated by a mediator either to assist in the mediation or to communicate with the participants in preparation for a mediation."

It is important that you clearly understand what these definitions mean and how the words used in this code section can potentially affect your family law case. Therefore, let's analyze this code section a bit further by giving meaning to what we just read.

Neutral to Process, Impartial to Outcome

A mediator is neutral to the process. While the mediator will likely be a family law attorney, the attorney mediator does not represent either party. The mediator is assisting as a mediator, *not* as an attorney. This seemingly small distinction is actually very important.

When a lawyer "represents" someone, there is a duty of loyalty and zealous advocacy owed to the client. As such, the attorney must protect and advocate for the client. Likewise, the attorney cannot take any action that conflicts with his or her client. In mediation, the attorney mediator has no such duty to either client. Instead, the attorney mediator in family law mediation is assisting *both* parties, and the attorney mediator should not be advocating for either party.

Another important concept to understand is that a mediator is impartial to the outcome. The mediator is not vested in any particular result. Instead, if the parties agree on and understand the outcome, and the outcome happens to favor one party over the other, the mediator is under no obligation to make the outcome more balanced.

The same concept of transparency mentioned in the chapter on collaborative law also applies to mediation. There should be no "secrets" between the mediator and each party. To the greatest extent possible, all communications between the mediator and the parties should include all three of them, whether it is a phone call, an email, etc.

Mediator Is Facilitator, Not Decision-Maker

One of the main services a family law mediator provides to people is the facilitation of acceptable agreements between the parties. Unlike a judge or an arbitrator, if the parties continue to disagree over an issue, the mediator cannot make any rulings or orders. Additionally, the mediator cannot make recommendations to the court to aid a judge in making decisions for the parties.

The mediator cannot make any decisions for the parties. All substantive decisions made in mediation must be made by agreement between the parties, and it is one of the mediator's primary responsibilities to help the parties reach those agreements.

So, you may be asking: "What happens if we continue to disagree on something?" If there is no agreement on an issue in non-adversarial resolution, whether it is a collaborative law case or a mediation case, then that issue is brought into court for a judge to decide.

"Acceptable" Versus "Fair" Agreements

The mediator assists the parties in reaching *acceptable* agreements, not *fair* agreements. The importance of this distinction cannot be overemphasized, and if you are considering mediation as a non-adversarial process to resolve your family law matter, you should have a very clear understanding of this distinction.

Essentially, laws are promulgated to provide fairness. Think about how the law is applied to various areas. In criminal law, a convicted criminal may serve time in jail or may need to pay a fine for something like a DUI or a speeding ticket. In contract law, maybe someone is ordered to pay an amount of money that would have been paid but for a breach of contract. In tort law, a defendant may be ordered to pay a sum of money to the plaintiff for lost wages as a form of restitution. In these examples, we think of these outcomes as being "fair."

Likewise, the laws that apply to California family law cases are also meant to be fair. Therefore, in applying this line of thinking, we can say that a "fair" outcome in a family law case is what the law would provide. Since a judge is required to apply the law to your facts, you could also say that a fair outcome is what you would expect to receive if you went to court. However, what if parties agree to a different outcome…an outcome that is different than what a judge would decide—an outcome that is different than what the law would provide—would that be "fair"?

Earlier in this book, you read about how a non-adversarial process could help you control the outcome of your case. As a refresher, remember that with most family law issues, if the parties are not in front of a judge, they can choose to deviate from what the law would likely provide. For a more detailed review, please refer to the chapter *"Choosing a Resolution Category."* If the parties both agree to an outcome that is likely different than what the law would provide, then this outcome is labeled "acceptable."

If you define "fair" as "what the law would provide," then such an agreement would not be "fair." Therefore, a mediator helps people reach acceptable agreements, which might be different than what a judge would decide.

Other Mediators Potentially Involved

As stated in Evidence Code Section 1115(b), a "mediator includes *any* person designated by a mediator to either assist in the mediation *or* to communicate with the participants in preparation for a mediation" (emphasis added). As with collaborative law, various professionals may be incorporated into family law mediation, such as a neutral financial specialist or a child specialist. Perhaps a family friend is brought into the mediation to provide some assistance, or maybe it is a church member that both parties trust.

Side Note: For reasons that will be discussed later in this chapter in the section titled *"The Family Law Attorney Mediator,"* I *strongly* recommend that your "primary" mediator is a family law attorney.

Regardless of who the additional person is that is involved in mediation—whether a professional or not—if this person is "designated by [the] mediator to either assist in the mediation or to communicate with the participants in preparation for a mediation," then that person is also considered a mediator. As such, the rules of mediation apply to these individuals as well, including mediation confidentiality, which I will now discuss.

Confidentiality in Mediation

In California, there are many safeguards that protect both the parties and the mediator in terms of keeping certain aspects of the mediation confidential (if you reside in a different state, consult with a family law attorney mediator in your area to learn about confidentiality laws in your area). Having these safeguards in place gives the parties and the mediator peace of mind that they can speak freely without fear that something could later be used against them. This allows for more open communication and greater likelihood that issues can be settled. The following are highlights of confidentiality in California mediation that you should become familiar with.

California Evidence Code Section 1119 states:

"Except as otherwise provided in this chapter:

(a) No evidence of anything said or any admission made for the purpose of, in the course of, or pursuant to, a mediation or a mediation consultation is admissible or subject to **discovery**, and disclosure of the evidence shall not be compelled, in any arbitration, administrative adjudication, civil action, or other noncriminal proceeding in which, pursuant to law, testimony can be compelled to be given.

(b) No writing, as defined in Section 250, that is prepared for the purpose of, in the course of, or pursuant to, a mediation or a mediation consultation, is admissible or subject to discovery, and disclosure of the writing shall not be compelled, in any arbitration, administrative adjudication, civil action, or other noncriminal proceeding in which, pursuant to law, testimony can be compelled to be given.

(c) All communications, negotiations, or settlement discussions by and between participants in the course of a mediation or a mediation consultation shall remain confidential" (emphasis added).

Breaking this down into layman's terms, this means that nothing said during a mediation session or even a mediation consultation is admissible or subject to disclosure, including an admission. This is powerful stuff!

The same protection that applies to something stated orally also applies to a *writing* that is prepared for, or in the course of, mediation or a mediation consultation. So you can understand the breadth of the term "writing," Evidence Code Section 250 defines a "writing" as "handwriting, typewriting, printing, photostating, photographing, photocopying, transmitting by electronic mail or facsimile, and every other means of recording upon any tangible thing, any form of communication or representation, including letters, words, pictures, sounds, or symbols, or combinations thereof, and any record thereby created, regardless of the manner in which the record has been stored." As you can see, a "writing" includes quite a bit. Note, however, that certain family law forms required by law to be filed are *not* confidential.

Broadly stated, all "communications, negotiations, or settlement discussions" must remain confidential, whether oral or written. Arguably, almost anything stated in mediation or in a mediation consultation will fall into one of these categories. The legislature clearly wants to ensure that confidentiality is applied widely to mediation so people feel comfortable speaking about issues without fear that something can be used against them later.

The Mediation Team

The minimum number of people involved in family law mediation is only three: (i) The mediator and (ii) the two parties. That being said, similar to collaborative law, there is great flexibility in bringing additional professionals into the mediation process, provided everyone agrees. I will now discuss, in more detail, (i) the family law attorney mediator, (ii) consulting attorneys, and (iii) various other professionals involved in mediation.

The Family Law Attorney Mediator

You may have noted in the section "*Authority for Mediation*" that there is no requirement that mediators have any special training or hold a special license. A mediator is simply a neutral participant that facilitates agreements between people in order to help them arrive at mutually acceptable agreements regarding issues in dispute. Arguably then, almost anyone could be a mediator…an attorney, a therapist, a church counselor, a family member, a friend, etc. So then, *who* should be your family law mediator?

If you are facing a family law issue, such as a divorce, there is no doubt that you should hire a family law attorney to sit as your mediator. The following are several important reasons you should retain a family law *attorney* to be your mediator for your family law **matter**. These reasons can be lumped into two types of assistance a family law attorney mediator provides to people: (i) *Procedural* help and (ii) *substantive* help. Let's explore these concepts now.

Attorney Mediator: Procedural Help

Let's say a divorcing couple agrees on everything in their case (ahem…not likely). There are still many *procedural* questions to be dealt with: "What forms do we need to file?" "*How* do we file forms with the court?" "How do we properly **serve** forms to comply with State law and constitutional due process?" "What are the various timelines involved in a divorce case for things such as the California 'cooling off period'?" "What are the various filing fees required by the court?" The list goes on.

A family law attorney will be able to assist with these types of issues. Typically, it is the family law attorney mediator that handles such things as filing forms with the court, serving documents on the parties and preparing documents on behalf of both parties. There truly is an art to correctly preparing family law documentation, and family law attorneys have the knowledge and experience to do this. Also, an attorney will be aware of any additional documentation that is required by your local court. Therefore, the procedural assistance, alone, provided by a family law attorney is invaluable.

A family law attorney handles family law procedural issues in his or her daily practice. There are many pitfalls that can occur in family law cases. One mistake could be very expensive to correct, if it even *can* be corrected. You want your case to be done right the first time around. Any time you do not use a family law attorney to assist with the procedural facets of your case, you are taking a serious risk.

Attorney Mediator: Substantive Help

Substantive help refers to the facilitation of agreements between the parties on all of the issues that are involved with a family law case. For example, in a divorce case where there are minor children, some of the issues to discuss include **property** division, spousal support, child custody and child support. It goes without saying that all of these issues are legal in nature.

Throughout your family law mediation, it is critical that you are educated and informed so you can make thoughtful decisions. A family law attorney mediator can provide what is called the "**shadow of the law**." In other words, the family law attorney mediator can explain the law for various issues. For example, a family law attorney mediator can provide information to the parties about California community property law, spousal support, child custody and child support. Once you hear how the law works with these various issues, you can make informed decisions and come to a resolution that is comfortable to you.

In my opinion, making informed decisions goes to the heart of why non-adversarial resolution is successful. Think about it. Do you know of anyone that actually *wants* to go to court, to be continuously stressed out because of not knowing what a judge will decide, and to spend thousands or tens of thousands of dollars on an attorney to help ensure a "win" in court? So then, why do people go to court? One of the main reasons is because they think the judge will give them something *better* than what they are hear being offered by the other party.

As an example, let's say you are going through a divorce and you have minor children. *You* would like *sole* custody of the children, and the *other parent* would like *joint* custody. If you both feel the law is "on your side," then you both will be more likely to go to court to get "what is fair."

However, what if you both chose a non-adversarial form of resolution, such as mediation, and you were both informed that, based on your case, a court would likely award you both with *joint* custody. Additionally, let's say you chose to hire a consulting attorney and, in speaking with your **consulting attorney**, the attorney confirmed that the court would likely issue a *joint* custody ruling—echoing what the mediator stated. In this case, you would probably be less likely to bring your case to court and ask for *sole* custody since—from what you are hearing—you would likely receive *joint* custody, which is what the other parent is requesting.

Side Note: For more information on consulting attorneys in mediation, see the section titled *"Consulting Attorneys in Mediation"* found later in this chapter.

The point being made with the above-mentioned example is that knowing the outcome you would likely receive in court may assist you in settling out of court, which can save you quite a bit in fees. In mediation, a family law attorney mediator can help you understand the law, which will help you settle your case out of court.

Finally, a family law attorney mediator has something that can only be acquired through time and doing something over and over again...experience. As a family law attorney, the mediator has likely seen many successful resolutions for a particular issue. After all, this is his/her livelihood! Therefore, the family law attorney mediator can offer potential solutions that worked for other cases for an issue where you and your spouse have reached an impasse. Oftentimes, the mediator will mention a solution that you would not (and could not) have thought of on your own.

Family Law Attorney Mediator Background

You may be wondering whether it is better to choose a family law attorney mediator that *only* mediates, or whether to choose a family law attorney mediator that *also* has a litigation (i.e., court) practice. There could be pros and cons to both. If there is a family law attorney that mostly litigates and only performs very little mediation, then it is possible that this attorney mediator does not have the same skill set as a full-time or frequent-practicing mediator. At the same time, a family law attorney mediator that also handles litigation has additional insight over a family law attorney mediator that only mediates and does not handle any litigation. The following explains how an attorney mediator that also litigates can be a great asset.

The law is not always black and white. There are often many grays, and judges are oftentimes given a very wide amount of discretion to resolve issues. As such, judges are people too, and they sometimes have their own tendencies or beliefs with respect to certain issues. There could be local custom shared by the judges in a one area that differs from another area. Litigating cases also requires a current knowledge of family law since the law will need to be argued in court. If the family law attorney has experience litigating these gray or highly discretionary topics in front of a particular judge or a courthouse where your case will be filed, then this attorney could likely offer a good guess as to what a judge may rule with respect to the law as it applies specifically to your facts.

For example, maybe Judge Jones tends to issue rulings of shared custody, and rarely issues sole custody. Hearing this opinion may influence your negotiations if, for instance, you have children and your case would have been heard by this judge had the case been brought into court.

Consulting Attorneys in Mediation

Unlike collaborative law, in mediation there is no requirement that either party must hire an attorney.

Indeed, it is certainly possible that the parties simply meet with the mediator and not have any independent legal representation throughout the mediation process. However, either party may, at any time, hire a **consulting attorney**.

A consulting attorney's services are much more limited when used in connection with family law mediation. First, the consulting lawyer does not become a party's **attorney of record**. This means that the parties still represent themselves. It is the parties' names—not the attorney's name— that are inserted in the **caption** (i.e., the top) of any legal paperwork.

Second, consulting attorneys do not typically attend mediation sessions. Instead, a consulting attorney is in the background, waiting to be contacted if needed. The attorney is available to be called upon by a party to answer questions, and to review and provide feedback on documentation prepared during the course of mediation. If parties prefer to have their attorneys active in the case, such as attending mediation sessions, then the parties should choose collaborative law instead. In such a case, why pay a mediator and two attorneys in mediation when you could just pay two attorneys in collaborative law?

You may be asking why someone would want to hire a consulting attorney. First, a consulting attorney—unlike a mediator—is looking out specifically for the client's best interest. A mediator is neutral; a consulting attorney is not.

Second, a consulting attorney can provide great peace of mind. For example, let's say you craft a global settlement agreement in mediation. You can (and should) bring this agreement to your consulting attorney to review and provide feedback *before* you sign the agreement. The consulting attorney may have suggested revisions; maybe the consulting attorney simply reviews the agreements to ensure you understand them; or maybe the attorney indicates that all looks okay. Either way, you will likely feel more comfortable in signing the agreement.

Third, a consulting attorney is a great sounding board. For example, let's say you are involved in a divorce action and you just finished with a mediation session where you discussed the very complex and emotionally-charged topic of spousal support. If you hire a consulting attorney, you can inquire as to whether your attorney has any additional thoughts regarding spousal support that you would like to bring to the table at a future mediation session.

I once heard a statistic that people only retain about one-third of what an attorney states. For particularly complex issues, such as spousal support, I believe it is helpful to hear information more than once. After all, repetition is the mother of skill—the more you hear it, the more you will likely remember it. Therefore, if you speak to your consulting attorney about topics you know you will be addressing in future mediation sessions, it will likely help you to feel more assured in your decisions.

Side Note: As a reminder, due to the many roles an attorney may take in a family law matter, I have created an *Attorney and Therapist Role Chart* to clearly display these roles. The *Attorney and Therapist Role Chart* can be viewed in Appendix A of this book.

Other Professionals Potentially Involved In Mediation

Other professionals may be brought into the family law mediation process, provided everyone agrees. By "everyone," I mean the mediator and both parties. For example, any of the professionals mentioned in the chapter titled *"Collaborative Law"* can be used in mediation, such as a communication specialist, a child specialist or a financial specialist. Additionally, experts can be brought into the process as necessary and agreed, such as real estate appraisers, business valuators and accountants. Even non-professionals such as a family friend could be brought into mediation.

Depending on the facts and circumstances of your case, the family law mediator may suggest the use of other professionals. If so, both you and the other party must agree to involve these other people in mediation.

CHAPTER FOURTEEN: A LITTLE ABOUT RETAINERS

Side Note: For ease of reading, in this chapter, the term "attorney" includes the term "mediator," since the material applies to both attorneys and mediators. It is also assumed throughout this book that a mediator is a family law attorney.

Oftentimes, family law attorneys get asked the following questions: "So, how long do you think my case will take?" "How much will my case cost?" These questions present the attorney or mediator with challenges, both on a professional and an ethical level.

First, assuming a **flat fee** structure is not offered by the attorney, these questions cannot be answered with any accuracy. This is because most of the factors that influence time and cost are outside the attorney's control. The three largest factors are: (i) Complexity of the case, (ii) how well the parties cooperate with each other, and (iii) the "approach styles" of the parties. These factors were previously discussed in detail in the chapter titled *"Factors That Influence Cost."*

Of course, the potential client wants to hear that the case cost will be low and that the case will be over quickly. Let's say the attorney provides an estimated total cost for the case or an estimate for the amount of time the case will take. These figures then get fixated in the potential client's mind. If the attorney does not deliver as "promised"—meaning either the case took longer than quoted time or the case is more expensive than the quoted cost—the client will be dissatisfied with the services received. On the other hand, if the attorney provides a conservative estimate for time or money to avoid the potential for under-delivering, this may turn away business. Due to the foregoing, some attorneys, including me, will simply discuss hourly rates, **initial retainers** and **renewable retainers**, without quoting numbers for time or money.

Most of the time, family law attorneys will require an initial retainer. Many family law attorneys will also require a "renewable retainer." Therefore, it would behoove you to learn about them so you understand how they work. Let's explore initial retainers and renewable retainers now.

Initial Retainers

The **initial retainer** is an amount that the attorney receives up front in order to begin working on the case. This amount is not "earned" by the attorney yet. These funds still belong to the client, but the attorney holds these funds in a trust account. As the attorney earns fees or needs to pay **costs**, such as court filing **fees**, the attorney draws funds from the client's trust account. Depending on the nature of the service (i.e., full service litigation, partial service litigation, mediation, collaborative law, etc.), the complexity of the case and the attorney's hourly rate, an initial retainer can be several hundred, several thousand, or even tens of thousands of dollars. While the billing cycle can vary, attorneys in family law commonly bill their clients on a monthly basis.

It is important that you understand that the initial retainer is *not* a flat fee, nor is it a guaranteed amount the case will cost or even an estimate of how much the case will cost. A **flat fee** is a fixed cost charged by an attorney for a certain service, regardless of how long the service takes. Flat fees are not typical in family law due to the many factors outside the attorney's control that make a flat fee impractical. Be very careful if an attorney or mediator quotes a flat fee for any family law issue.

Many legal insurance plans provide a flat fee to an attorney for various services, and most of the time the flat fee paid is extremely low considering the amount of time the attorney puts into the work. Be careful with legal insurance plans. Consider the following:

Let's say an attorney's hourly rate is $250. XYZ Legal Aid Company has a contract with this attorney/mediator that you, as a client, pay $1,000 as a flat fee for a divorce action. This is four hours of time at the attorney's normal hourly rate ($250 x 4). Now, let's say the attorney reaches eight hours or more of time in your case. This means that the attorney has now earned $125 per hour ($125 x 8 = $1,000). The more time the attorney spends on the case, the lower the attorney's hourly rate becomes.

Now, ask yourself: How happy is the attorney going to be once (in this hypothetical) the case goes beyond four hours? It goes without saying that the attorney likely prefers working on a case that will earn fees closer to his or her normal hourly rate versus working on a case that continues to reduce the normal hourly rate.

Renewable Retainers

In family law, renewable retainers are very common. A **renewable retainer** is also called an **evergreen retainer** or a **replenishing retainer**. This is the minimum dollar amount for a client's trust account that must be maintained throughout the case.

As an example, let's say you are quoted an **initial retainer** of $5,000 and a renewable retainer of $2,500. When you provide the signed fee agreement to the attorney, you provide the initial retainer payment of $5,000. Over time, the $5,000 will decrease due to case **costs**, such as court filing **fees**, as well as payments made to the attorney for earned fees.

Let's say your retainer drops to $2,000. In this example, you would then need to replenish your retainer back to $2,500 by providing the attorney with an additional $500.

Let's say the retainer drops to $1,000. You will then need to provide the attorney with $1,500 to get your retainer account back to $2,500. At the end of your case, any unearned funds in your retainer account get refunded to you.

Simply stated, both initial retainers and renewable retainers help assure (i) payment to the attorney for fees earned, and (ii) that case costs can be paid, such as court filing fees and court runner fees. Similar to the initial retainer, the amount of the renewable retainer will largely be dependent on the type of service chosen (i.e., full service litigation, partial service litigation, mediation, collaborative law, etc.), the complexity of the case, and the attorney's hourly rate.

When you are consulting with an attorney, whether for litigation, collaborative law or mediation, be sure you understand the attorney's fee structure, including the attorney's hourly rate, initial retainer amount and renewable retainer amount.

CHAPTER FIFTEEN: TIPS TO HELP REDUCE COSTS

No matter what resolution option you choose, whether it is **mediation**, **collaborative law** or **litigation**, there are steps that you or the other party can take to help mitigate the cost of your case. The following are some tools that may help reduce costs in your case.

Tip # 1: Utilize a Joint Expert

Whether you are in an adversarial or a non-adversarial mode of resolution, if it is determined that an expert could be helpful or necessary to shed light on some issue in your case, consider using a **joint expert**. A joint expert is neutral and does not advocate for either party. While **costs** for a joint expert can be apportioned as agreed, most of the time the joint expert's fees are shared equally by the parties.

When a joint expert is hired, there is one opinion that is typically just accepted by the parties. On the other hand, when there are two experts (i.e., one expert for each party), it is common for the results of the experts to be different, which can actually foster more litigation and lead each party to concretely believe that it is "his" or "her" expert's opinion that is the correct opinion. Additionally, it goes without saying that two people paying for one expert is likely going to be less expensive than the parties each paying for their own experts.

Oftentimes, there are experts that are known in your legal community. A family law attorney can suggest names of experts that have a good reputation in your local area.

Tip # 2: Obtain Counseling to Remove Negative Emotions

A mental health professional's assistance can be invaluable during a family law **matter**. Family law issues typically carry heavy negative emotions. Negative emotions and logic are like oil and water— they do not mix. Picture a small room with one window. If negative emotions and logic are in the room, but they both cannot fit, it is logic that typically goes out the window, leaving the negative emotions behind. Negative emotions cause poor and rash decision-making.

A mental health professional can help tame and diffuse negative emotions, replacing logic in their wake. While there may be costs associated with counseling sessions, there is a good chance that the money spent on counseling will save hundreds or thousands of dollars in case costs because there was more cooperation and productive communication that occurred.

If you are like most people, assuming your case is not a "happy" one like an adoption, you will experience a myriad of negative emotions throughout your family law case that could adversely impact your case, such as anger, depression and hurt feelings. A therapist can provide great assistance through a divorce or other family law issue where negative emotions are common. Additionally, there is a good chance that the tools you learn can be applied to other areas of your life, extending their use well beyond your family law case.

Another consideration for visiting with a therapist is cost. While attorneys are "counselors" of law, most attorneys do not have specialized training in behavioral health. Attorneys are trained to think logically. On the other hand, a therapist is specifically trained in behavioral health. Additionally, you could likely pay a therapist less in fees to help you with an emotional issue versus your attorney.

The cost of therapy may also be a covered benefit through your health insurance plan. If you feel that professional emotional support could be helpful, check to see whether therapeutic services are covered by your insurance. Whether or not therapeutic services are covered by your insurance, speaking to a therapist about the emotional aspects of your case will likely be cheaper than doing so with your attorney.

Tip # 3: Obtain Training to Communicate Productively

Many relationship problems come down to poor communication, and I am not talking about just intimate relationships. I am also referring to parent/child relationships, employer/employee relationships, relationships between friends, and other personal relationships. Maybe we jump to a false assumption. Maybe we verbally attack someone when we do not intend to do so. Maybe we *hear* what someone else is saying but we are not really *listening*.

People typically mean well when attempting to communicate with or listen to another human being. However, the truth is that many of us have not learned how to communicate productively and non-defensively. There are resources out there for productive and non-defensive communication, including books, audio books and therapists.

Be open to suggestions provided by the other party and keep the concept of "**reactive devaluation**" in mind, which can be reviewed in the chapter titled *"Factors That Influence Cost."* Learning good communication tools may be just the ticket to have an efficient and successful family law case. Additionally, productive communication tools will likely benefit other relationships in your life, which makes the investment a wise one.

Tip # 4: Obtain Training on Child Development

If your case involves a dispute over minor children, it may be helpful to obtain training and education regarding child development. For example, the needs of children with respect to their parents are different at six years old versus sixteen years old. Children go through several developmental phases from the time they are born until they turn eighteen. Parental behavior impacts children differently at various ages. The need and length of time for children to be physically in the care of their parents changes with age.

If you learn about and understand (i) child development in general, (ii) child development for a child the same age as yours, and (iii) specifically where your child is developmentally, you will be more likely to approach custody and parenting time in a manner that will be most beneficial to your child.

Tip # 5: Accept "What Is"

"What is" is something that simply "is." In your case, the other party is his or her own person and you have no control over this person. This is one example of "what is." As such, it is advisable to respect your differences with the other party, which may include a different parenting style. Realizing that there are certain things in life that you cannot change is actually quite liberating. When you realize that you cannot change what is, and that the only person you have complete control over is yourself, your approach will likely change for the better.

Sometimes our ego takes control where we do not even realize that we are taking actions that attempt to control another person. Bringing these actions to a conscious level, you can realize what your ego is doing and begin to "go with the flow" rather than try to control someone else. Doing so will likely help you approach your case with more flexibility, and with more relaxation.

Tip # 6: Stay Present

When we are in the present moment, we step out of time. We step out of the past, which can cause emotions such as anger, resentment and sadness. We also step out of the future, which can give rise to emotions like fear, worry and anxiety. The past oftentimes leads to blame: "If he/she did this differently, we wouldn't be getting a divorce!" The future often takes away our joy of the present moment because we are focused on something occurring in the future to either bring us joy, or maybe we are thinking about something that may happen in the future that makes us feel sad, mad or scared.

Focus on the here and now. You will likely enjoy life more, and answers come easier when our mind is not flooded with incessant thinking about the past or the future.

Tip # 7: Focus On Win/Win Solutions

If it seems that you and the other party are at an impasse, try to come up with alternate solutions that are win/win scenarios—good for each of you. A mediator or attorney could be very helpful with impasse breaking techniques. It is likely that the attorney or mediator has confronted your issue or a similar issue in the past and successfully helped other clients overcome the issue. If so, the attorney or mediator could have a quick and easy fix if the same solution is acceptable to you.

Many issues in family law have many possible solutions—you just have to continue to look for them. Sometimes our ego gets in the way and we focus on and get entrenched in our position so we can "win." We only see one way that works.

Asking yourself good questions can help you arrive at good answers. For example: "How can I alleviate the other party's concern and, at the same time, not sacrifice my own values and still get what I would like?" "Is there a solution to this that I'm not seeing?" "What opportunities are here that I haven't noticed before?" "What is funny about this situation?" "How can I go through this process and have fun at the same time?"

Coming up with win/win solutions not only allows you to potentially keep your case from being decided by the judge, it can save time and fees in the long run since both you and the other party will be satisfied with the outcome.

Tip # 8: *Research Potential Attorneys*

Side Note: For purposes of this tip, the term "attorney" includes the term "mediator."

Putting your case into a professional's hands— whether it is a litigation attorney or family law attorney mediator—is no small and inexpensive task. You want to have the utmost confidence with your attorney, and you want to feel comfortable with the attorney. With the internet, you can learn a lot about attorneys by visiting their websites. Maybe there are videos where you can get a better sense of the attorney. Maybe there are testimonials. Maybe you can speak to someone who was previously assisted by the attorney. What is the attorney's training and background?

Whatever you can find, you should consult with an attorney before signing a retention agreement. Some attorneys may not provide you with a fee agreement unless and until you have had a consultation because they are interviewing the clients, just like the clients are interviewing the attorney. In any case, a consultation will give you a great opportunity to see how you feel about a prospective attorney. A consultation will not only give you a good sense of the attorney's competence, you will also get a sense of whether your personalities gel, which I believe is an important component of any professional relationship.

You should think about questions you would like to ask the attorney and then bring them with you to the consultation to ensure that you do not forgot to ask something that is important to you. Do not be afraid to ask a question, even though you might feel uncomfortable. After all, you will be placing quite a bit of trust in—and spending a good amount of money on—a professional to help you with sensitive and important issues.

Do not be afraid to consult with more than one attorney before making a final decision. It is hard to measure something unless you have something to measure it against. If you consult with more than one attorney, you will likely have a better idea as to which professional you feel most comfortable with.

CHAPTER SIXTEEN: CONCLUSION

Filing a family law action with the court is a big decision. It is not something that anyone looks forward to doing, unless it is a positive matter, such as an adoption. The decision to file for a divorce, for example, is of a similar degree as the decision to have children, to get married, or to buy a house. Likewise, there are many unknowns and there are no guaranteed outcomes. Much of the stress in family law actions comes down to fear of the unknown. Therefore, the more educated and informed you can become, the more you will feel at ease.

One of the most critical decisions you can make in approaching a family law action is to determine what *resolution option* you feel most comfortable with. Are you interested in mediation? Collaborative law? Litigation? It is also common for people facing a family law issue to be concerned about how much the case will cost if a professional is involved.

It is my hope that this book has provided you with education and information to guide you towards choosing a resolution option, and that you have learned some tips and tools along the way to reduce acrimony and to mitigate costs. For more information about Ginter Family Law, various family law issues, family law self-help tools and much more, visit Ginter Family Law on the web at **www.GinterFamilyLaw.com**. Feel free to look at the information together with the other party if you are comfortable in doing so.

From Ginter Family Law, I am family law attorney and mediator, Bryan Ginter. I wish you the best.

APPENDIX A: ATTORNEY AND THERAPIST ROLE CHART

Due to the number of roles an attorney and mental health professional can assume in a family law action, the next page contains a graphical chart that clearly displays these roles. Please note that some of the names of the roles are specific to California. If you do not reside in California, you should consult with an attorney to determine what the names of the roles are as used in your local area.

Bryan C. Ginter, J.D.

ATTORNEY AND THERAPIST ROLE CHART
By Bryan C. Ginter, J.D.
(Non-Exhaustive List)

	ATTORNEY	THERAPIST
MEDIATION	1. Mediator for any legal issue. 2. Co-Mediator 3. Consulting Attorney	1. Mediator for custody and/or parenting time issues only 2. Co-Mediator 3. Communication Specialist for one or both parties 4. Co-Parenting Counselor 5. Reunification Counselor
COLLABORATIVE LAW	1. Attorney for one of the parties	1. Communication Specialist for one or both parties 2. Child Specialist 3. Therapist
LITIGATION	1. Full Service Attorney 2. Partial Service Attorney 3. Consult-Only Attorney	1. Therapist 2. Communication Specialist for one or both parties 3. Child Custody Recommending Counselor 4. Custody Evaluator 5. Psychological Custody Evaluator 6. Co-Parenting Counselor 7. Reunification Counselor

GLOSSARY

The following words are defined by the author as they are meant to be applied in this book. The definitions for these words may be different than the generally understood meaning of the words. Note that some of the terms apply only to California. If you reside outside of California, you should consult with an attorney in your area to determine the applicability of these terms to your jurisdiction. For example, the term "community property" may not apply to you if you reside in a "separate property state."

- **Adversarial Resolution Category:** There is no formal written agreement in place that the parties will keep their case out of court and refrain from implementing various litigation tools. Either party may bring the case into court at any time.

- **Attorney of Record:** When an attorney represents a client and most, if not all, communications are directed to the attorney instead of the client. Everyone, including the court, is put on notice that the client is represented by an attorney and who that attorney is.

- **Bench Trial:** When a trial involves the judge sitting as both the judge and the trier of fact. There is no jury.

- **Caption:** The top of the first page of a legal document that includes the following information: The parties' names, the contact information for the attorney that is filing the document, the case number, the title of the document, and the court where the document will be filed.

- **Case Law:** Law that is provided by upper level courts, including state appellate and supreme courts.

- **Caucusing:** An impasse breaking tool sometimes used in family law mediation and collaborative law. It is when the parties are physically separated into two or more separate rooms. The mediator then sits with each party individually; if it is a collaborative law case, the attorneys travel back and forth between each other to discuss issues.

- **Characterization:** Whether a particular piece of property is one party's separate property, all community property, or some combination of community and separate property.

- **Code(s):** Also called "statutes," they are laws provided by a state legislature. An example is the California Family Code.

- **Collaborative Law/Collaborative Law Process:** An out-of-court process in family law where the two parties each have their own attorney. A series of meetings take place until all issues are resolved. Typically, the collaborative law agreement that is signed states that all professionals must be fired if the process fails for any reason.

- **Confidentiality:** The concept that a writing or oral assertion cannot be made admissible as evidence for consideration by a judge, nor can the writing or oral statement be communicated to third parties.

- **Consulting Attorney:** An attorney that may be hired by a party undergoing family law mediation to provide advice and feedback throughout the process. This lawyer does not become the party's "attorney of record" and the attorney is typically not present during mediation sessions.

- **Co-parenting Counseling:** A service provided by a mental health professional to teach parents tools to be able to positively communicate with each other regarding the care and upbringing of their children.

- **Costs:** Consists of "fees" and "expenses."

- **Court Formula:** Law + Facts = Order or Judgment.

- **Court Runner:** A person hired by an attorney or mediator to file documents with the court on a party's behalf.

- **Curriculum Vitae:** A professional resume.

- **Discovery:** A formal tool used in legal proceedings to acquire information and documentation.

- **Dissolution of Marriage:** The modern term for a divorce. It is the termination of a marriage.

- **Equalization Payment:** In a divorce or legal separation action, it is a payment made from one party to the other party in order to equalize the division of community property when one party receives more in community property value than the other party.

- **Evergreen Retainer:** See "Renewable Retainer."

- **Expenses:** Charges incurred in a family law case for such things as court filing costs and court runner fees. Essentially, these are costs that do not consist of fees paid to an attorney or mediator for professional services rendered.

- **Fees:** Funds earned by an attorney or mediator for professional services rendered.

- **Flat Fee:** A fixed cost charged by an attorney for a particular service, regardless of how long the service takes.

- **Hearing:** A court proceeding where parties and their attorneys appear in court and present issues to the judge for decision. Typically, the length of a hearing is fifteen minutes or less, sometimes called a "short cause hearing."

- **Initial Retainer:** The amount required by an attorney or mediator to begin work on the case.

- **Irreconcilable Differences**: One of two grounds in California that support a divorce or legal separation action. It is when the marriage is over in either party's mind with absolutely no chance of repair.

- **Legal Separation**: If a legal separation is granted, the parties' marriage remains intact. However, for tax purposes, the parties may no longer file jointly.

- **Litigation**: The status of a matter when there is no formal written agreement in place stating that the parties will keep their case out of court and refrain from implementing various adversarial tools.

- **Joint Expert**: A single expert hired by the parties to a case. Oftentimes, the parties equally share in the costs of a joint expert. This expert is neutral and does not owe a duty of loyalty to one party over the other party.

- **Jurisdiction**: The county of the court where your case will be filed.

- **Long-Cause Hearing**: A lengthy court hearing.

- **Mandatory Settlement Conference**: A court-required meeting at the courthouse with the parties and their attorneys shortly before a trial or long-cause hearing for the purpose of reaching a settlement and avoiding the upcoming court appearance.

- **Matter**: A legal proceeding that includes one or more family law issues to be resolved, including, but not limited to, dissolution of marriage, child custody, child support and property division.

- **Mediation:** An out-of-court process to resolve a family law issue where both parties meet with a neutral person (i.e., the mediator) in a series of meetings until all issues are resolved. The mediator facilitates agreements between the parties and also prepares and processes legal documentation.

- **Non-Adversarial Resolution Category:** There is a formal written agreement in place stating that the parties will keep their case out of court and refrain from implementing various litigation tools. The two non-adversarial methods discussed in this book are collaborative law and mediation.

- **Nullity:** Also called an "annulment." If the court grants a nullity, the legal effect is that the marriage never existed.

- **Parenting Plan:** A writing that contains provisions related to legal custody and physical custody of minor children, including which parent makes decisions regarding the children's health, safety and welfare, as well as when the children will be in the physical care of each parent.

- **Party(ies):** Someone involved in a family law dispute that is named in a legal proceeding as either the petitioner, respondent or claimant.

- **Preliminary Settlement Thoughts:** Ideas (not agreements) that are arrived at by the parties themselves without professionals involved that may resolve any number of issues currently in dispute. These ideas are then discussed with professionals involved, such as attorneys or a mediator, to determine whether any of the ideas will be incorporated into a formal agreement that will be filed with the court.

- **Premarital Agreement:** Also called a "prenuptial agreement." This is an agreement made in the contemplation of marriage. A common reason premarital agreements are used in California is to avoid various applications of California's community property law.

- **Pro Per:** Also called "in pro persona." It is when a party does not have an "attorney of record." The party represents himself or herself in the family law matter.

- **Process Server:** A professional who formally provides legal documentation to someone involved in a legal proceeding in a manner that complies with due process of law.

- **Property:** Assets—both real and personal—and debts.

- **Reactive Devaluation:** A form of negative conditioning that occurs when there is a communication breakdown between two parties such that a proposal or suggestion by one party is automatically discounted or disregarded solely because it was stated by the other party.

- **Renewable Retainer:** A minimum amount of funds required by an attorney or mediator to be maintained in the client's trust account throughout the duration of the case. Also known as an "evergreen retainer" and a "replenishing retainer."

- **Replenishing Retainer:** See "Renewable Retainer."

- **Retainer:** A certain sum of money provided to an attorney or mediator that is held in trust for a client. As the attorney or mediator earns fees or incurs costs on behalf of the client, draws are made against the client's retainer. See "Initial Retainer" and "Renewable Retainer" for specific retainers discussed in this book.

- **Reunification Counselor:** A mental health professional that assists in strengthening the relationship between a parent and a child.

- **Serve:** See "Service of Process."

- **Service of Process:** The formal process of providing legal documentation to the other party in a way that conforms with due process of law.

- **Shadow of the Law:** A term used in family law mediation when a family law attorney sits as the mediator. This describes the process of being educated on various family law topics and to receive an opinion as to what may occur if the case were to be brought before a judge.

- **Statutes:** See "Codes."

- **Subpoena**: A written request to produce documents and/or for a person to appear on or before a set time and at a particular location.

- **Trier of Fact**: Someone who decides what facts are true in weighing admissible evidence presented at a trial. In California family law trials, the judge also sits as the trier of fact. In other areas of the law, such as criminal trials, a jury is the trier of fact.

- **Web Meeting**: A meeting conducted over the internet with the ability to see and hear other attendees who have joined the meeting using their own devices that connect to the internet. Documentation can also be uploaded to the virtual meeting space and viewed by all attendees.

INDEX

Made in the USA
Middletown, DE
12 October 2021

50179455R00093